WITHDRAWN

No longer the property of the
Boston Public Library.
Sale of this material benefits the Library

T3-BNJ-763

Black America:

An Economic Powerhouse in the Dark

Black America:
An Economic Powerhouse in the Dark

By

Eric Franey

Nova Science Publishers, Inc.
Commack

Art Director: Maria Ester Hawrys

Assistant Director: Elenor Kallberg

Graphics: Denise Dieterich, Kerri Pfister,
Erika Cassatti and Barbara Minerd

Manuscript Coordinator: Sharyn Beers Schweidel

Book Production: Tammy Sauter, Benjamin Fung
Christine Mathosian and Joanne Bennette

Circulation: Irene Kwartiroff and Annette Hellinger

HC 110
·C 6 F 73
1996 b x

Library of Congress Cataloging-in-Publication Data
available upon request

Copyright © 1996 by Nova Science Publishers, Inc.
6080 Jericho Turnpike, Suite 207
Commack, New York 11725
Tele. 516-499-3103   Fax 516-499-3146
E Mail Novascil@aol.com

All rights reserved. No part of this book may be reproduced, stored in a
retrieval system or transmitted in any form or by any means: electronic,
electrostatic, magnetic, tape, mechanical photocopying, recording or otherwise without permission from the publishers

Printed in the United States of America

DEDICATION

This book is dedicated to the two most important women in my life--my wife, Melva, and my mother, Barbara. Thanks for your unwavering love and support.

CONTENTS

About the Author

Eric Franey is president of Franey Inc. advertising, marketing, and public relations, based in Little Rock, Arkansas. His firm specializes in ethnic advertising and marketing for large banks, corporations, and government agencies.

In addition to being an advertising executive, however, Franey is also a screenwriter, model and actor, having most recently appeared in the HBO Movie, *Tuskegee Airmen*, starring Laurence Fishburne, Malcolm Jamal Warner, and Cuba Gooding, Jr.

Franey's varied skills also enable him to serve as a consultant, strategist, account manager and creative director.

His prior professional advertising and marketing experience was with a large, prestigious general market advertising agency, where he performed the multi-state advertising function for a multi-billion dollar Fortune 500 corporation.

Eric Franey holds a degree in marketing, and is a graduate of the University of Arkansas at Little Rock.

Franey is a visionary. He has made many predictions, which he has seen virtually all come to pass. In fact, since this book was published, you may likely notice that some of his predictions have already come to pass. Perhaps, it is only a matter of time before his other predictions do too.

INTRODUCTION

Undoubtedly, a book like this will mean many different things to many different people. But at the same time, and regardless, this book contains something for everyone--general interest readers, marketers, business persons of all sizes, politicians and laymen alike. All can gain something valuable from reading this book.

This forum addresses many key issues from a largely broad marketing perspective, and this perspective is very important. However, it should be understood that marketing and business initiatives are not this book's only application, nor direction.

This book also enters into the relevant, but sensitive areas of political and social discussions as well, enabling it to be used as a spring board for many varied applications. But nonetheless, hopefully, this book will begin to focus much more deserved attention on important areas and the important African-American "market."

So to that end, we will address golden opportunities, information you should know, and information you must know to "do it right." The benefits, not the liabilities of affirmative action will be discussed, and the significant impact which politics has on these discussions will be addressed as well. As you may see, all of these issues, in one way or another, are deemed very important when attempting to market to, be sensitized to, or understand certain issues relating to today's African-Americans.

However, while it is intended that you enjoy your reading of this book, note that its purpose was not designed to pacify the egos of anyone, black, white, brown, whatever. Its content is frank, candid, real, and very straight-forward. So, for anyone who is looking for ego pacification, or warm and fuzzy discussions during periods where business is frenzied, coupled with political and social chaos, you may have the wrong book. But for those of you who wish to be enlightened, well-informed, sensitized, and the like, then you will likely be glad you read this book.

But before we go on to our analysis, talk of guerilla marketing assaults, discussions about politics and the like, it is important to note that hopefully, this book will be a call-to-action for many, as I hope many will take notice, dive-in, and make their contributions to this and other important, noteworthy areas.

I want you to know up-front that in some instances, you may have to take my word for some things, based upon my personal and professional first-hand knowledge, years of research, analysis, and continuing experience in the field.

But for those who will inevitably come out of the woods, and who would like to do nothing better than to criticize this and other such information, for whatever political purposes it may serve, note my invitation to positively contribute, and write your own book.

As far as this book goes, while it is not intended to answer every single question, it should be seen as great information, an excellent bench mark, and a great start for many people looking to expand, positively advance, and the like.

So having said all of that, I hope you enjoy your reading of this book, and here's commentary.

Eric Franey

BILLION DOLLAR
BUSINESS OPPORTUNITIES

The Bottom Line

First, let me start by stating that even though I wrote this book, I am a businessman first. This is simply stated to let you know that I did not write this book just for the sake of writing a book. I would not waste your time with such trivial pursuits. However, as we are embarking upon some very important times: economically, politically, socially, and all of the above, I wanted to bring some rather important considerations to the forefront. However, if you have not already done so, then I recommend that you read the preceding introduction before moving on.

First, as American businesses continue to focus on developing thriving new markets around the world, many companies are missing-out on untold billions of dollars right here at home. For right underneath our noses, markets exist which can be considered a marketer's dream. And one such market in particular, is the African-American market.

Ironically, though the opposite may be assumed, too few persons actually understand the significant economic impact the African-American market has on companies' bottom lines. And even fewer persons truly understand the actual buying power versus the perceived buying power of this group.

Most companies do not know how to approach this market, and some still are not sure why they even should approach this market.

This keen lack of awareness, among other things, traditionally has caused many to shun the African-American market as a viable means to profits. But as you may have heard the old cliche', "What you don't know *can* hurt you," it certainly could not be more true in this case. Today, we are in a new age, and I can assure you that continuing to shun this market, would not be a wise move for anyone to make.

The retail industry has recently begun to realize this fact, and entities such as financial services institutions are following suit by beginning to pay close attention as well. The reason? Because the economic impact of Black Americans is very astonishing, though many are only just now becoming convinced. Others, however, are still not yet quite convinced. So, my simple words are, for those who wish to survive into the competitive future, by all means, do not underestimate Black America.

The first thing that I propose *any company* do, is to first evaluate its customers closely. The reason is because even if a company thinks it knows who its customers are (probably based upon a nine year-old survey), the sheer lack of awareness still prevalent today, indicates that obviously, many companies do not. Most companies would be shocked to find out that some of their bread and butter customers are low to middle-income blacks, a group which most entities have traditionally shunned.

This will likely hit most organizations right away, as they recognize that they have not done very much to court the business of blacks, but know from recent discussions that perhaps they should. And many organizations would also likely be even more amazed if they reviewed the income profiles of some of their "actual" bread and butter customers, coupled with what these people really think about their company. This would likely create shock waves, and I do not necessarily mean shock waves for the better.

Well Eric, I'm hard-headed. I hear you, and I recognize that some other companies are doing this, but I'm still not convinced that I should court the black market, you say? Well, figure this into your intellectual equation. With competition getting significantly stiffer in just about every type of business these days, and with sharp declining demographic numbers on the part of the "general market," companies must begin to do a better job at paying much closer attention to ethnic markets. If not, because of stiff competition in the general market, coupled with the changing shifts in demographics, which is making blacks one of the largest growing populations in America, companies will have little choice but to see general market customers, sales, and profits decrease in the near future if they do not court ethnic markets.

But if an organization is resistant to such changes, then it should start saying its prayers, because if its lucky, before it's all over, a company will come along and buy that company for a bottom-out price, as many "big fish" are doing today. And this would naturally happen just before they go into Chapter 7 bankruptcy, of course. Are you with me so far? I hope so.

To most companies, there are a lot of unanswered questions about ethnic markets, the black market in particular, which has grown to more than $300 billion in annual buying power. And in case you haven't conceived just how large an amount that is, you should note that it is larger than the annual budgets of most small countries. It is larger than the annual operating budgets of most of America's largest cities, combined. It's nearly twice the amount the U.S. government spends annually on goods and services ($180 billion). Why it is even more than 75 times the size of the large, industry-leading, multi-billion dollar, Fortune 500 company I used to perform the advertising function for. So in other words, Black America is a real economic powerhouse.

However, with this much economic clout, why are so many blacks today begging for diversity from Corporate America? One reason is because Black America is truly an economic powerhouse *in the dark*.

Let's Be Real

In keeping with my promise of not patronizing anyone, wasting your time or mine, let's address the *real* issues. One of the first subjects which we will address is the subject of American blacks and whites doing commerce together.

First of all, we must say phooey on words like "diversity" and other such patronizing and patsy sounding terms. We must also say phooey on persons who over-use these words, and who are afraid to state their cases, rather than calling it like it really is. We do not have that kind of time to waste.

So listen friends, let's opt not to play coy any longer. Each year, many organizations around the country hold conferences and fairs to showcase black businesses to major corporations, and show what these businesses have to offer.

Many times, these corporations actually show up, because such fairs are great opportunities for corporate public relations. But virtually never, are any contracts awarded at or as a result of these fairs and conferences. The author has personally attended at least a half-dozen of such conferences and fairs, and always has left with the same story to tell. That story? While the author appreciates the talent and dedication which goes into making these fairs possible, out of the scores of corporations which have been made aware of talented, qualified, professional black-owned businesses, ready to work with their company, the author has seen not one single contract awarded. Instead, one prevalent outcome seems to evolve--black business owners walk away feeling blue. Now what does this tell us? It tells us a lot.

First of all, it tells us that most companies could care less about buzz words such as "diversity," or the legal consequences associated with not hiring or contracting with blacks. So we'll quickly cut to the chase. Doing business with blacks in the U.S. is really about three things: Money, power and racism. And as you may realize, when we finally stop with the cute sounding buzz words, and start addressing things for how they really are, some rather interesting assessments and analysis can be made. Such a focus is the direction, scope and intentions of this book.

Changes In The Marketplace

As we know from several research studies, Black Americans are not only consumers, but from that perspective, are one of the largest consumer groups in the entire country, are the largest minority group in the entire country, and are the largest consumer group in many important product categories.

The sad irony, however, is that despite the large amounts of money that blacks spend with most companies, in upwards of $300 billion yearly, many companies have not represented black's spending with near equal levels of employment, contract opportunities, promotions to management level positions, etc., despite ample evidence that they should.

Now an argument could be made that this should not necessarily be the case. And I do hear you, but try telling that to a group who spends nearly $300 billion each year on consumer goods, and see if that argument does not run into deaf ears.

Essentially, what I am saying is that many companies have simply ignored, or in many ways, disrespected some of their bread and butter customers, a marketing taboo. This has been done for insignificant reasons at times, and other times, for no reason at all. Many organizations have just presumed that blacks will simply continue to do as blacks did in the past, and continue to buy companies' products, because they have little choice but to do so. However, as this obviously does not sound like a wise assumption, it does bring us to another discussion.

Historically and traditionally, blacks simply spent their money with white-controlled companies. Blacks received little in return, and gave little thought to the economic stimulus process, or the economic clout which they wielded.

This was a large reason why blacks were only seen limitedly on television during the early 1980's. In fact, until the late 1980's, it was still sometimes possible to watch television all day, and never see any black people in commercials. Why? Because most companies believed that blacks would simply buy their products, regardless to whether they were marketed to or not.

Recently, however, this pattern has noticeably begun to change. Why? Do blacks still do business with companies who do not market to blacks? Many do. So did companies suddenly gain compassion for blacks, and thus begin to feature more blacks in print ads and on television and radio, for diversity's sake, compassion or humanity? Hardly. So why did blacks suddenly begin appearing on television, in print ads, and on the radio? Because most organizations simply began to realize increases in the amounts of money they were making by targeting black consumers. And as a result of making more money, today, we have companies spending hundreds of millions of dollars to reach black consumers.

In the past, many organizations which often had terrible track records for hiring racial minorities, and those who for long periods of time, even delivered terrible service to blacks, were still often able to secure significant amounts of black business, with little or no effort.

But to make matters even more interesting, in many instances, large numbers of blacks purposely avoided doing business with other blacks, just so they could do business with whites, as some even do to this day. There were many reasons for this syndrome, but many experts will tell you, especially my Ph.D friends, that this has its roots dating back to the infamous U.S. Slavery Period--No wonder why American slavery was often called the "peculiar institution."

As my Ph.D friends would also continue to tell you, blacks often behaved in such a manner, because many had been trained to believe that doing business with whites would give them increased status or clout, or had some sort of premium attached. This was how many blacks had come to be conditioned, and most white-owned companies acted accordingly.

I do not state this information to give you a history lesson. However, I state this for a higher, more practical reason. I wish to inform you that within Black America, for many reasons, things have changed--and are continuing to change. In fact, things are changing so much today, that I virtually come with a warning.

Whether you are a business person, small or large, politician, interested citizen, or whatever, you should note that today, something is happening within our country. It cannot necessarily be seen, but it can be felt. Some things are still very unclear, but one point is for certain--a new generation has surely been born.

This fact will undoubtedly come to mean many different things, but one thing which this fact means for sure, is that the old days of doing business is no longer acceptable. This is not to suggest things like some African-Americans will not remain prey to past, unfortunate thinking, or that all businesses will change, because undoubtedly, some things will remain the same. But companies and individuals should take notice that on a large scale, the game is changing fast, and for the most part, so are the rules.

Now, while some may brashly assume that many people already know several things about Black America, perhaps many do. However, as you may or may not be surprised, from this author's numerous experiences, *many* people know very little about this group, and in many instances, even those who think that they know much about "the black marketplace," often times know too little to be overwhelmingly effective.

Why Things Have Changed

As a group, blacks have traditionally been undisciplined, slow and unorganized when attempting to mobilize groups of people to action on important issues. The institution of slavery, then followed by decades of forced segregation, marginalized black people so much, that many blacks even began to marginalize themselves.

This was so as what were once referred to as the "Slave Codes," lingered, and were rigidly enforced, meaning that blacks were often swiftly and severely punished for even minor offenses. They were legally forced from being educated, they could not own weapons, or assemble crowds of more than three blacks at a time. During slavery, these "codes" also ensured that even free blacks were to be treated as inferiors to poor whites. Perhaps you can notice some similarities between these codes of yester-year, and the behavior often espoused by many whites today.

You see, quite frankly, black people today are in a chess match where the competition is cheating against them. Blacks know that the competition is cheating, and also know that the competition will continue to cheat. As such, it would be unintelligent for blacks to continue playing under the same circumstances, and many blacks have awakened to this fact. What should blacks do? Perhaps the only logical thing--pick up their marbles, and find another game to play. So regardless, this is the overview of the situation between American Blacks and their relationship with White America.

But hold on, blacks are not cheated by whites, you say? Then explain why in cities all across America, as blacks and whites both pay taxes, why is it that roads always seem to be bumpy in black neighborhoods, yet are almost always flat and smooth in white neighborhoods?

In many instances, blacks are not mayors, and many are not city directors, etc. And the result of this is that the needs of blacks are often neglected. Their tax dollars often go to benefit white neighborhoods, ultimately white residents, and white and women-owned (non-black) companies in the form of contract awards. But rarely do black neighborhoods, black residents, and black-owned firms benefit. This is reality. Take a look at the following statistics compiled by the U.S. Census Bureau.

Minority & Women-Owned Businesses:

	1987	1992	% Increase
Women-Owned	4,114,787	**5,888,883**	43%
Black-Owned	424,165	**620,912**	46%

The actual five year numerical increases for women-owned (non-black) businesses from 1987 to 1992 was 1.8 million, but for black-owned businesses, it was less than 200,000. Also, cash receipts by women-owned firms increased by more than 131%, and less than half of that for blacks, during the same time period.

Blue Collar Construction Companies:
Construction Firms Owned By **Racial Minorities**

	United States	% Increase
1972	39,875	
1987	**107,650**	**169.9%**

Construction Firms Owned By **Women**

	United States	% Increase
1972	14,884	
1987	**94,308**	**533.6%**

(Source: U.S. Census Bureau)

Note: Women-owned construction businesses nearly doubled between 1987 and 1992.

Now, while I am a fan of women-owned businesses, I also recognize that many women who classify themselves as minorities, and who have few if any barriers to obtaining or raising capital, are benefitting at the expense of black-owned businesses--many who have great difficulties in obtaining or raising capital, and securing contracts. This is evident by looking at the numbers, and also helps to explain why 56% of all black-owned businesses had gross cash receipts of less than $10,000.

Few more than 3,000 black-owned businesses had sales of $1 million or more in 1992. However, "Angry White Males" claim that they are being victimized. Looking at these numbers, if white males are being victimized due to affirmative action, it certainly is not at the hands of blacks. Wouldn't you agree?

So, armed with these figures, as this is the case, where has Black America's $300 billion yearly incomes gone? Obviously not to black-owned firms. The fact is that most of black's earnings went mostly to white-owned companies who didn't respect blacks enough to even advertise to them. But wait. As the above statistics are alarming, was this author the first to stumble upon them? Hardly. So why hasn't more been done to correct this obvious major problem? The answer is because many of the advocacy groups charged with getting black companies business, are supported by corporate dollars. Therefore, these organizations and individuals cannot afford to "rock the boat." Why they virtually have their hands in the back pockets of the companies, persons and organizations with whom they are disgusted with, and many large companies wish to keep it like this, because it's safe for them. But, this is also like selling your soul to the Devil too. Thus, this is a good reason for a black attitude change.

You see, the true essence of power for black people is not in creating or advancing individual wealth. For if one black person becomes a millionaire, that is great. However, if a large firm or wealthy individual dislikes him for whatever reason, and wishes to see him fall, if they have substantially more money than he or she, how difficult is it to drag this individual into court on trumped-up charged, and make him spend all of his money defending himself against persons or entities with tens of millions, hundreds of millions, or even billions of dollars? It would easily break him. Remember the once multi-millionaire O.J. Simpson?

This is stated to simply and obviously assert that group wealth must be considered as the only viable alternative for Black America's prosperity into the future, not individual wealth. And this concept must be practiced, and not just preached, because for those who do not practice it, over the long-term, they will surely hurt *themselves*. This is because if an individual has "made it," yet his brother has not, then that individual too has not made it.

He must keep his mouth shut, and do not rock the boat because he has no one to stand with him. He must "stay in his place," no matter how much wrong, human suffering or corruption he encounters. This continuous vicious cycle has literally paralyzed Black America.

So, all of this is stated to say that Black America should not begin spending more of its wealth with black businesses to create a few black entrepreneurs who become wealthy. While that is great, the real reason why Black America *must* do business with black businesses, is because all blacks are *powerless* without this being the case.

Please allow me to explain. Until tens of thousands, hundreds of thousands, and/or millions of black-owned businesses and black organizations have gained economic independence from Corporate America,

Black America will have to continue to pander to these companies, and essentially sacrifice its core beliefs, dignity, and black prominence, by remaining inactive. Until blacks retain economic independence from corporate dollars, blacks cannot support politicians which they might like, but corporations do not like. Blacks also cannot engage in any activities with persons or organizations which corporations do not like... And just think, some blacks thought they were free.

The truth is that most blacks feel backlashed by most whites today. However, this situation, has in many ways, begun to turn a negative into a positive. This means that though our current social climate is unfortunate on one hand, almost seeming to punish blacks after the O.J. Simpson Trial. On the other hand, it has begun to unite previously non-unified groups, who had grown apart from one another, and thought they had less in common than they really did.

Many educated blacks, particularly those capable of executing decisive, military-style, social, corporate and political leadership decisions, in the past, often times thought themselves too prosperous to be confronted with the plight of most everyday, "common blacks," thus these people often shied away from "black causes" and "black issues." But today, however, many of these people have awaken to find themselves in a world no different than when they were "colored."

Many of these predominantly "middle-class," suburban blacks, today, find themselves in Corporate America, leaning to the "white side," but realize that they are not accepted as equals by their white colleagues, no matter how talented or "qualified" they might be. Many of these people are changing their minds by the thousands, as many have become "men without a country," returning to their black heritage only after having their humanity rejected by most whites. In other words, no matter how different the socio-economic backgrounds of well-to-do blacks, and common blacks, today, it is obvious that blacks are all confronted with the same basic situation.

While many of these people are returning to their roots, do not expect for these people to become leaders. As many abandoned the causes and beliefs of blacks once before, they will not be given that opportunity again. No, new leaders will emerge--disciplined, fierce, young lions, which will be smart and charismatic leaders. These young people will pick up the torch, whose flame has simmered for more than thirty years, and will lead blacks, likely under the guidance of the few, but older, wise, faithful blacks, who never abandoned them, or who never sacrificed their futures simply for a home in the suburbs.

Now, as a marketing professional whose job is to keep pace with the trends and changes of society and the marketplace, I am informing you that change is on the horizon.

As many rave about the recent decreases in crime statistics, and attribute this decline to the increase of more police on the streets, or stiffer sentences, I'd like for you to consider another theory. I wish for you to consider that maybe, just maybe, instead, this decline has much to do with the trend of changing attitudes among many young blacks on the streets, who before, might have been sentenced for committing black-on-black crimes, but who have today grown tired of black fractionalization, and non-unity among black people.

In fact, the only real negatives which keep blacks in a low-profile status today is drugs and black individualization, unlike Jews, Asians or Italians, who gained social acceptance by gaining economic respect. And with regard to drugs, ironically, more seem to be hitting our streets everyday. Gee, I wonder why?

So you see, change on the part of blacks, seems to indicate that perhaps, for the first time in American history, the horrible after-effects of slavery are finally beginning to wear-off. This means that many blacks are developing new attitudes, and that many are now shedding their old cloaks of dependency upon whites.

Many blacks are beginning to recognize their own strengths, and have begun to act accordingly, opening businesses despite being denied bank loans, producing new products, offering new services, and becoming more creative. And as with most people, once they have experienced being their own boss, rarely will these people ever wish to go back to the old days, and the old ways of doing things--being afraid to speak out, being afraid to do this, or being afraid to do that. These American liberties that blacks thought they had, but many now know differently, are helping black people awaken to understand the difference between the realities of freedom from the illusions of freedom.

History professor and House Speaker Newt Gingrich summed it up nicely when he stated, "Throughout time, freedom has carried with it a great price tag. It has not just magically arrived for anyone. The persons or groups who have all obtained freedom, have done so by having great courage."

Now, while you reflect upon the above powerful phrase, I will leave you with New Hampshire's official state motto, "Live Free or Die."

Ethnic Marketing Is Big Business

As we discussed earlier, sure, ethnic marketing would likely be great for public relations. Heck, it could even be considered a wonderful gift for mankind, or "diversity." But really, the bottom line here is that regardless, marketing to black people is not really about any of these things. It's about business, big business. So, if anyone is reluctant about this fact, then I have a grim prediction for that individual, or his or her organization in the future--such a person or entity will likely fall far-short of its hopes, dreams, and aspirations, and that, you can virtually bank on.

The purchasing power of blacks for many years has been grossly, and I do mean *grossly* underestimated, under-appreciated, and all of the above. But rightly or wrongly, these attitudes have continued to follow blacks largely because of an almost oppressive, historical mood aimed at them. And being from Little Rock, Arkansas, I can attest to that. But anyway, with the recent rise of the educated black middle-class, a group consisting of high wage earners, doctors, lawyers, professors, advertising agency owners, politicians, professional athletes, engineers, journalists, administrators, entertainers, authors, film and television producers, agents, publishers, etc., a group which I give considerable praise to in this book, much more economic power then becomes realized versus what has been perceived by most individuals.

What does all of this mean? It means three things. First, most companies probably have wrong assumptions about just who their customers really are, and how much they spend. Secondly, a large number of most companies' customers are black, and these people often spend more on average than most companies' "general market" customers. And thirdly, most companies often wrongly assume that they have less black consumer patronage, and more black consumer loyalty than they really have.

As you may know, stiff competition is probably here to stay. So what do you think would probably happen if your company's competitor launched a powerful ethnic marketing program that your company could have delivered, but didn't? That's right, your company would be placed in a reactionary mode, a bad position to be in when marketing products or services.

What do you think would likely happen to a non-progressive, ethnic marketing company's ethnic market share? That's right, it would probably take a nose dive.

So, while people might assume that on the average, whites spend more money in various areas because whites are a larger segment of the population, that does seem logical. However, what I am telling you is that assumption is not necessarily the case.

Yes, there are more whites than blacks in our society, and according to the 1990 census, nearly ten times as many white households earned incomes of $25,000 and up, when compared to blacks. However, in numerous areas, blacks still somehow out-spend and/or spend more on average for products and services than the general market. And this is true even despite such a wide gap in earnings. But, an additional hidden factor is the purchasing behavior of blacks compared to whites. This is something that most raw statistical data just doesn't deliver.

This factor demonstrates that many blacks have often purchased high-priced items that whites earning the same incomes do not purchase-- especially items related to prestige or status. One of the surface reasons for this syndrome is because, while whites earning say $25,000 per year can purchase a particular item, they often feel that they cannot afford an item, thus they do not buy. But many blacks on the other hand, who earn say

$17,000 per year, in fact may likely buy that item--whether it be a car, electronic item, dinner at a nice restaurant, whatever. One simple reason, is because blacks have been less concerned about financial uncertainties than whites. This was primarily because many blacks grew-up with less than financial security. As such, blacks traditionally have not worried about being able to afford something, versus being able to buy.

Notice my experience one afternoon while I was driving about town, simply observing for marketing purposes (the type of thing I do regularly). In a three hour drive-about, I observed eleven late model Mercedes Benzes ($45,000+ cars), being driven mostly by African-Americans. There were ten to be exact, driven by persons who were black, and only one did I observe who was white. Now, this is not to signify that only blacks drive Mercedes Benzes, and whites do not, but this is an example of how whites and blacks may earn the same incomes, but demonstrates the added willingness of blacks to spend their money on such high-priced merchandise.

However, I must pause for a moment. Let me just say here that if you earn $30,000 per year, financially speaking, you should not be driving a $30,000 car, a depreciating asset. This is America, and sure, people can do what they please, but being practical is important if one wishes to be a part of a growing economic powerhouse. And being a part of an economic powerhouse does not come by *spending* one's money, especially with companies who do not respect the customers spending those dollars.

And that statement drives me to an additional statement--the words of one successful Atlanta business executive, who I heard speak years ago, "If you wear something on your ass, it should not be considered an asset." This is good food for thought.

Relevant Comparisons

I have often driven through both affluent black and white neighborhoods, making comparisons. What I found in affluent white neighborhoods is that there were few expensive automobiles, except in more neon light type places such as Dallas, Texas for instance. But nonetheless, I noticed that most of the cars in affluent white neighborhoods were simply practical $15,000-$22,000 automobiles. And in these neighborhoods, when I did see expensive automobiles, most were at some of the smaller homes on the block. After further evaluation, the reason appears to be because most affluent whites are often conservative in nature, and simply see automobiles as mere forms of transportation, used to get from point A to point B. But in contrast, the majority of blacks I interviewed were more interested in the style, class and comfort of vehicles, thus many were in most cases, willing to spend more for vehicles/transportation.

In affluent black neighborhoods, I noticed many Lexuses, Mercedes Benzes, Jaguars, etc., and big homes too. This was very interesting to me, as I had just reviewed the demographic and income profiles of both blacks and whites in those neighborhoods--what I saw did not match the incomes.

In largely low-to-moderate income black neighborhoods, I often encountered expensive automobiles parked out front of small, sometimes dilapidated looking houses. Individuals seemed to wear almost the best fashions that money could buy--Nike, Reebok, Fila, Tommy Hilfiger... (incidentally, at the time of writing this book, Tommy Hilfiger's stock had tripled over the last few years, and the other companies mentioned all reported strong corporate earnings). But nonetheless, this scenario was quite a paradox, and as such, needs to also be addressed right here.

From the depths of slavery and oppression, black people rose, but in the process, many rose with a great need for feeling "I am somebody. I am not a slave." This deep emotional quest, over a century later, even sometimes for educated blacks, has caused many to become great consumers, and wish to buy the "best." For usually, when a person is deprived of something, as many blacks have been so often, people usually develop a great appetite for that item.

No matter how trivial the actions of purchasing expensive items may seem, to people who come from little, these things can appear to be monumental in giving some self-esteem, when before, persons were stripped to having none. And although I am a fan of moderate fiscal conservatism and deferred gratification, I do understand this plight. However, I am pleased to see that many blacks are becoming secure within themselves, and are putting away such potentially damaging mind-sets.

With time, one can notice this scenario changing, as blacks who once earned $50,000 per year, and who would have then purchased a condominium, a prestigious automobile, and wore the finest clothes that money could buy, all while having little or no bank account, is too becoming history. I applaud such changes.

Black America is indeed an economic powerhouse in the dark, and the only problem is that blacks are just now beginning to realize this fact. So, the only other question, which lies outside of the scope of this book, but will be included in my upcoming book, is how Black America can make the transition from being an economic powerhouse in the dark, to becoming an economic powerhouse in the light. This situation undoubtedly will soon make a favorable, timely presence as well.

Common Mistakes

Despite significant income gaps between blacks and whites, they continue to still buy roughly the same quantities and qualities of goods. But many companies do not know this type of information. For if they did, we would probably see far more African-Americans in the corporate work environment. I am also confident that many companies would seek to change corporate attitudes to those which have become necessary to securing the business of ethnic customers--if these companies only realized what large quantities of business they were really missing-out on.

Undoubtedly, even today, non-racially hospitable companies benefit from black customers. But the question which is posed, is how much are these companies benefitting? Are they benefitting as much as they could if they were more sensitive to the concerns and issues related to Black Americans? Will they continue to benefit in the future? The last of these three questions is perhaps the most important of all.

The fact is that most companies are likely benefitting far less than they would otherwise, regardless to how much African-American business they may presently receive. And if that amount is significant, then that company would likely do itself a huge favor by courting ethnic customers.

Briefly look at this example. African-Americans, who had only 1.3 million "affluent" households earning $50,000 or more in 1989, compared to more than 20 million white households for the same year, spent more than $250 billion on consumer goods in 1989. Now, assuming that your math skills are decent, this means that it is unlikely that blacks who earned $50,000 or more per year, by themselves, add up close to $250 billion, even if they spent every dime. Did you figure that much?

One inference which can be made from all of this, whether obvious or not, is that a very substantial number of African-Americans who buy companies' products, earn less than $50,000 per year. In fact, most earn *substantially* less.

Now, this factor should be significant to business persons, as often times, advertisers and marketers tailor their messages to those groups with household incomes of $50,000 or more. So what I am saying is that this is often a large, common mistake among many companies and advertisers when marketing to African-Americans.

However, another important point is this. Despite the approximate $280 billion spent by African-Americans in 1993, advertisers spent only less than half of 1% of that amount, or $800 million trying to reach them. And of that amount, only one-third was spent with black-owned advertising agencies.

Most executives believe that these numbers are too small to make a huge impact on the growing, thriving African-American market. This author agrees. So, if the data does not convey to you that the above inferences are correct, then based upon my expertise in this field, allow me to tell you that these inferences are correct.

Another inference which can also be made, with assistance from the figures listed in this chapter, and some listed later in this book, are that such a substantial difference between the numbers of "affluent blacks," compared to "affluent whites," despite educational attainments, indicates that many blacks are still being excluded from the fair hiring, promotion, and compensation processes.

Such information obviously would run counter to today's arguments heard by so-called "Angry White Males," but this is why education is necessary.

So, as we have only just hit the tip of the iceberg in this forum, we will continue to analyze many issues regarding business, marketing, economics, politics, etcetera, and couple those things with the many why's and why not's, all associated with Black America being appropriately called, an *Economic Powerhouse In The Dark.*

Important Information When Marketing To African-Americans

The Most Important Rule

Perhaps the most important rule of business when marketing to today's group of better-educated, more sophisticated, aggressive African-Americans, is regardless to what your personal views may be regarding blacks, you may want to re-evaluate your attitudes and opinions quickly. Why? Because a variety of issues affect African-American's buying decisions. And many are quite different from whites, as prejudiced attitudes and feelings about blacks, means that companies have likely just lost the race before it has even gotten started.

If someone wishes to understand, effectively and/or adequately capture the attention of the

African-American consumer market, or any ethnic market for that matter, then they must first understand a variety of issues. And to understand certain issues, persons may likely need to be sensitized accordingly. So, from time to time, please bear with me in this regard.

The days of doing business as in years past are over, as big fish are busy gobbling up little fish in mergers, acquisitions, and the like. In fact, in the banking industry alone, of the more than 10,100 banks in the U.S., the well-respected accounting firm of Deloitte and Touche, one of the big six accounting and consulting firms nationwide, predicts that as many as 50% of the nation's banks will soon be swallowed up by larger banks in the next few years. This adds to the already $40+ billion and climbing, in mergers and acquisitions involving banks.

Experts caution that this phenomenon is not necessarily good news for consumers, who could find these larger institutions suddenly unwilling to make "riskier" loans. Also, experts warn that these banks could simply wish to have less of their loan portfolios concentrated in areas such as real estate, for instance, creating an environment to where these banks might no longer issue loans to various individual customers, businesses, or otherwise--even if their payment histories are good.

And whether inside the industry of banking, or outside, those companies "in between" all will soon be squeezed out, unless they can find a niche. So quite simply, as today's business climate is more competitive than ever, the difference which Black America will make during this fight for survival, is that it will make the distinction between companies who stay in business, and companies who go out-of-business.

What Is Known

Several key issues currently affect the feelings and emotions of American blacks, but mind you, not all blacks are affected in the same manner, nor are all blacks considered "black" by blacks. But for the large majority of blacks, various things often stimulate and/or drive decisions to buy--or not to buy. So as such, these things are what we will candidly discuss.

If you're a business person, then you likely understand that for today's companies who wish to thrive, and even simply survive into the next millennium, there are a few markets which look very handsome for future business opportunities--and a few which look quite bleak. As we know from sources such as the author of the best-selling *MegaTrends 2000*, and most recently, *Global Paradox*, author John Naisbitt, Japan is expected to have only slow to moderate growth. Europe appears to be a no show in the upcoming race, despite all of its talk about a one currency system. And as much talk has praised it, Latin America certainly looks promising, along with Asia, as countries like China are at the forefront for instance. These are largely the downsides of the global investment picture. The upside, however, is that regardless, one greatly overlooked market is the ethnic market in the U.S., the African-American market in particular. For in the U.S., for most companies, this virtually untapped market is like a thief in the night, waiting to exhale.

As an example, let's say that today, a company has a large volume of black consumer-related sales, likely not as much as it could have, but let's say nonetheless, that the numbers are substantial. Now, whether you realize it or not, because of a myriad of competition, coupled with a virtual negligence by that company to appropriately address certain social and economic concerns, tomorrow, suddenly, most of that company's black customers are gone. Believe me, that's when company presidents would learn the value of, and feel the pinch of losing black customers.

So, in the near future, the Black American market will be key and likely more crucial than ever to most U.S. companies. Competition is growing more and more intense, and domestic financial concerns are growing more worrisome everyday. This will of course, eventually make consumer spending slow down, and coupled with the layoffs of millions of middle-class managers and professionals, many of them non-blacks (many black, largely hourly employees have resided at the bottom, due to lack of promotions and opportunities, thus they are less likely to be considered "fat," unlike mostly white salaried workers, and become unemployed middle managers), then these things all will make the "virtually recession proof" African-American market ironically even more attractive in the future.

But regardless, as the margin for marketing errors grows less and less, companies will have to wake up, take notice, and most importantly, take action.

In one way or another, the black market will be vital to the success of U.S. businesses, and even entire industries. So be prepared, because ready or not, Black America is well on its way to emerging as an economic powerhouse. The wheels of this machine are ready, all they need is simply a little "greasing."

Why There Is Little Competition Within The African-American Market

Presently, there is a serious lack of *effective* marketing aimed at African-Americans. And the reason for this lack of effective marketing aimed at African-Americans is three-fold.

1) Largely because Madison Avenue doesn't understand this market. It has been slow to react. Instead, it has continued to focus on its "comfort zone"--big mistake! No wonder some advertisers are moving their advertising away from Madison Avenue to non-traditional locations.

2) Many companies have the preconceived misconception that the black consumer market has little or no real buying power, thus they figure this market to be less than important (Perhaps one may see now that actually, quite the opposite is true).

3) Even though blacks are being marketed to, their senses are often not really appealed to, as white ad agencies, eager to make more dollars, usually are the one's hired to reach black audiences, often unsuccessfully. This should come as no surprise, however, as this carries the same logic of hiring an Asian-American agency to target hispanic customers--it's illogical.

For years, talk had surfaced surrounding the African-American market as a great possible market "niche" of the future, but what marketers did not realize then, was what some realize now--the African-American market was a sleeping giant, and collectively, was far larger than what had originally been thought to be the case. You see, this market is segmented in much the same manner as the general market. You have your small, prominent elite, a very sizable middle-class, and a less fortunate under-class, consisting of low wage earners, and at, below, or near the poverty line individuals.

Now, hanging-on to what was presented earlier, one should note that when one is talking about blacks, today especially, one is not necessarily talking about under-educated poor people. Sure, too many blacks are under-educated and poor, but then again, one under-educated poor person is too many.

But today, more college-educated blacks and black professionals exist than at any other time in U.S. history, shattering all stereotypes and myths, and more scholars and professionals are turning-out everyday, at least until Congress decides to pull the plug on certain types of education funding, which is already being attempted covertly. According to the U.S. Department of Education's National Center for Education Statistics, as of 1993, more than 1.4 million blacks were enrolled in colleges and universities. At least 58% were enrolled in 4-year colleges and universities.

Approximately 3 million blacks currently have college degrees. More than a half million have master's degrees, approximately 100,000 have Ph.D's, and approximately 100,000 have professional degrees, such as lawyers for instance. And of course, all of these people are coupled with the more than 4.5 million blacks who have at least some college under their belts, with several hundred thousand of these people being well-read, self-educated persons with master's degrees from the University of Experience. But regardless, despite black's educational and social attainments, unfortunately, many of their incomes still do not match their educations, intellects, nor the incomes of whites with the same levels of educations and experience. In fact, many blacks with college degrees still earn less than whites with only high school diplomas. So are blacks and whites really considered equals?

Previously, little information was really known about African-Americans and their economic profit potential. But as social concerns about Corporate America have been rising, for many companies, effectively tapping the African-American market today, can be a lot tougher than one might expect.

You see, marketing to African-Americans can be a very rewarding and very financially profitable experience. But with a new age of African-Americans, if such marketing is not done properly, attempts at penetrating this market could be devastating. One should understand that this market is essential for more reasons than just the obvious, and companies must understand much more than just the products or services they sell, if they plan to be competitive, or even survive into the upcoming, competitive future.

Take for example this book. As this particular book is aimed not only at African-Americans, but also general interest readers, politicians, and business persons, I am also busy compiling another book of its kind, aimed at specifically reaching Black Americans. The later of these two books will be an interesting highlight of information African-Americans in particular should know about the present and upcoming future. Hopefully, it too will be very informational, and widely read, of course.

But anyway, with such a book, traditional distribution avenues may be appropriate. However, as even in the area of book publishing for example, where there are still few African-Americans involved in the editing, marketing, and decision-making process, many well-known publishing houses even, do not fully understand the best ways to market books to ethnic audiences.

For instance, when marketing a book aimed at blacks, one should not necessarily just instantly assume that the book should simply be marketed through your average, mainstream book store. The reason? Many chains often are not well-educated in black book marketing, except recognizing when a book is making profits. However, without the proper knowledge, making those profits could prove difficult.

But nonetheless, one must analyze this situation on a case-by-case basis. So, as such, and with a heightened awareness of people supporting minority-owned businesses these days, among other concepts, surely other avenues will at least have to be considered. After all, with the exception of heavily black- populated areas such as Washington, D.C. and Atlanta, GA, how many African-Americans did you see at the mainstream book store where you likely bought this book? If the answer fits with the norm, probably not many. And one can bet that these low numbers are not an indication that blacks don't read, but are in some way related to the preceding comments.

Am I stating that African-Americans do not go into mainstream bookstores? Of course not. I am simply saying that companies should not be so quick to overlook the details, and should think the issue through first. You see, a long-running, yet diminishing perception among many publishers and individuals, is that African-Americans do not read. This perception is diminishing because black book sales, black magazine sales, more visible black professionals, college graduates and scholars, and a large, educated black middle-class, all seem to suggest that such a perception is far from the truth.

So, if one does not understand ethnic markets, that is fine. But one should probably recognize their own limitations, and thus at least seek the assistance of a professional organization which does, such as a skilled, professional ethnic marketing agency.

Now, while blacks are buying more books than ever, from this author's every observation (and these are numerous), many African-Americans often buy books from places outside of the "mainstream," such as college and university book stores, stores which specialize in African-American paraphernalia, black magazine offers, and even on street corners--not *necessarily* just giant mainstream bookstores. And believe it or not, such marketing often tends to work very well, as today especially, an increasing number of blacks are likely to support these books, surprising lagging mainstream expectations. So, this is just one example of many, to illustrate that when a company is selling products to African-Americans especially, other issues must be given as much consideration as the product itself.

Understanding Ourselves

Let's face it, we all know that some things happened in our nation's past, and many of them do not make us proud. However, we must move forward, and I'm sure you agree. But in order to positively move forward, we must first address unresolved conflicts such as race matters, for as these issues remain on the table, they cannot afford to remain unresolved, be avoided, or swept under the rug.

In many instances, throughout this book, the issue of race must be addressed candidly and openly for discussion. Hopefully, this will not bother you. And for most readers, this will likely be fine. But it should also be noted that in order to effectively overcome certain ethnic marketing hurdles, it is imperative that many people be sensitized, at least those who wish to be sensitized. And whites in particular, must overcome the reluctance to discuss issues and matters pertaining to race.

For example, take the average white person, and put them in a calm discussion with a black person. Everything will likely run smoothly. But the moment the black person brings up anything about race, no matter how non-derogatory, usually, the white person will turn uncomfortable. Why?

Understandably, many whites do not wish to feel guilty for the sins of ancestors, even though some of these ancestors are still living and are among us today. But in order to feel truly liberated from such forms of guilt, first, whites in particular, will have to begin by swallowing the reluctance to open up their minds and hearts, and dialogue about race matters. This is essential, and it's the only way to positively move forward. If we do not wish to do this, then none of us should question why a cloud of racism continues to hang over us.

As an intelligent business person, or informed citizen, one must clearly understand that there is no shaking it, we all do bear some responsibility in our current sad state of race relations. And though many whites hate to hear it, yes, to a large degree, blacks have been victims in our society, as many Americans viewed it better to have a class beneath them, rather than be considered at the bottom of the totem pole themselves.

This was the case in our nation's history once before, when poor, young white men from the South, rushed to fight and die to preserve slavery for those mere 20% of wealthy whites who actually even owned slaves. This same rationale is also why some even today, are still avid supporters of race suppression in our society.

So yes, racism is a part of our past, and unfortunately, it still hinders us today, but regardless, we must accept that no one can change the past, but we *can* shape our future. And in case you're wondering why I singled-out only whites, it is only because whites have largely been the most reluctant to discuss race matters with people other than whites. This is probably because many whites fear that whites have the most to lose, enjoying their social pecking order positioning. But as such, this is almost the equivalent of refusing to acknowledge that a rape victim has ever been raped, and in the process, telling that victim to get on with her life, without ever really consoling her. This is what the continued avoidance of healthy race-related communications with blacks is like. After all, America has never really truly lived up to, nor apologized for actions beyond mistreatment of blacks and the American Indian. So as such, how can we expect for America to really move ahead under these circumstances?

Sure, people understand that trauma caused by things such as rape affects persons psychologically, even though many of us have never been raped. However, many people often attempt to ignore that blacks have been raped--of opportunities, fairness, dignity, pride... And by doing this, in effect, people end up saying, "Yes, well, the plight of blacks has been tragic, but move on for Christ sakes." This without ever consoling blacks about the emotional scars that many still have, as would most people who have walked in black's shoes.

And for those who do not believe this, then turn your attention to millions of people who, once upon a time, earned $50,000, and even six-figure salaries with major corporations, but who now are desperately willing to work for $12,000, or are unemployed, and struggling to find the difference between themselves, and what they once called the average "bum" on the street. Many of these people are well-educated, 40+ year-olds, who felt it could never happen to them. But now, many know that they are being discriminated against because of their age, but what can they really do about it?

Sadly enough, many of these people are now about to walk in the shoes of many blacks, and perhaps those "bums" they once may have talked about. And needless to say, the picture doesn't look so optimistic for these people anymore. So, until a person walks in someone else's shoes, many times, it's difficult to identify with that person's plight. But we should remember that the world does continue to go around, for all of us.

In all honesty, race issues must be dealt with openly and fairly, despite the fear of opening up a can of worms. The reason is because racism has and continues to hurt many people, and if we do not progressively address this issue openly and fairly, and put a lid on it that way, then the issue will keep emerging, until soon, the can will no longer be able to hold the "worms."

I don't know about you, but I've never seen a favorable outcome arise when people ran away from an issue.

But anyway, another form of the "r" word, relating to some of my own personal experiences (and I could easily give you dozens), is when I was in middle and senior high school. I can remember dozens of young white girls, who all had crushes on black guys, but claimed that their parents were very prejudiced against blacks--and this wasn't too long ago. Many of these girls were from quite wealthy, and/or well-to-do, middle to upper-middle-class neighborhoods, so their dating black men was taboo. And needless to say, their romantic interests were often kept very low-profile.

The irony of all of this, was in seeing many of these girls years later in college, and beyond. I noticed what had become an apparent dislike for black guys from many of these women, all of a sudden. The way many of these girls acted towards black people in the general public would lead anyone to think that they in particular, surely never dated black guys--but they did. Many even fell in love, but because of such severe prejudice, often times felt but not seen, many of these young women routinely married rich white guys, moved to the suburbs, and began acting aristocratic in the presence of blacks. To sum things up, these women often kept their previous relationships between the select few blacks who knew, themselves, and the Good Lord. I can still remember the many negative thoughts that I suddenly had with regard to this apparent hypocrisy--and this was not just a couple of isolated incidents, I witnessed this time and time again.

This was not only the case with white girls and black guys, but it was also the case with black girls and white guys who desired them. However, ironically, often times, these same guys would "grow fangs" when they would see a black male with a white female. This is often the case in our society. Double standards are usually applied when comparing whites to the rest of the world, especially blacks.

While further seeking to understand ourselves, though they too endure discrimination, it can be argued that even hispanics are artificially placed in a higher social order than most blacks. This can be seen by the television stardom of husband and wife team, Ricky Ricardo and Lucille Ball. Both who were married and widely accepted during a time when it would have been strictly prohibited for the same to occur had Ricky been a black man. On a higher plane, the same can also be seen by the wide-spread respect and attention the business community has paid to the 22 million person, largely coastal city dwelling, $205 billion spending, Hispanic-American market. This is in comparison to the 30 million person, more widely distributed, $300 billion spending, less talked about, African-American market.

The author is not remotely suggesting that hispanics should not be marketed to aggressively. However, the author is suggesting that our current sense of direction should at least be re-examined.

But nonetheless, moving right along, the real problem with the double standards scenario listed earlier, was not necessarily the acts of involvement, but the "lily white," arrogant, almost anti-black attitudes that permeated thereafter. That was what this author found to be troubling, how about you?

We could easily go on all day with these types of examples, but the bottom line here, is that racism today isn't necessarily owning slaves, wishing to own slaves, or the like. Racism today exists in people's attitudes, in their mind-sets. It's the false-pride of "Hey I'm better than you," or "Hey I'm smarter than you..." It's believing or acting as if some people were born superior to other people, especially those who do not necessarily "look like us." Such attitudes are even more identifiable, when despite whatever educational or economic attainments some people might have, they are still viewed as slightly less than another person or group.

Racism is largely a psychological problem, which as the noted Dr. Cornel West stated in his best-selling book, *Race Matters* "...it's not just white people's burden, nor is it black people's problem." It is yours and mine, all of ours. And though I realize that this brief discussion may be unsettling for *some* right now, as you may see later, this slight discomfort now, may perhaps be more than worth its weight in gold to you later on.

In fact, while compiling this book, some people whom this author respects very much, advised me that perhaps I shouldn't address certain issues in this text. For they believed that some whites would not be able to handle certain discussions regarding race. These advisors believed that the sensibilities of whites might be offended, and that would somehow, cause this book to get a negative review.

I, however, dared to respectfully disagree, as I hope that this would not be the case. Therefore, I chose to leave certain material in, which I felt that most readers would appreciate knowing. Hopefully, I wasn't wrong. If so, then maybe we've got a longer way to go than I thought. But nonetheless, I guess only time will tell us for sure.

But anyway, for anyone who may be feeling discomfort right now, this is exactly one of the reasons why this book was written in the first place, so I hope you stay tuned.

But before I close this particular discussion, for those who may not know, if a person is white, they should not necessarily feel guilty for the actions taken by ancestors. However, people do need to be responsible for *their* actions. For insensitivity, in many instances, can be considered racist, which is a prime reason why racial tensions continue to still exist today-- insensitivity. And by all means, do not think that if a person has a black friend or two, that means that they are not a racist. The reality is, for some, that could mean just the opposite.

So lastly, people should just take note of these facts, and try not to have thin skin when discussing racial matters. It is not necessary, and as an old saying goes, "It does not matter where you come from, it's about where you're going." The sooner we all candidly deal with racial issues, across racial lines, the sooner we can all hopefully put these problems behind us, and make positive progress in a forward direction.

Where The Opportunities Lie

As growth rates in the general market continue to become flat, decline, or have only little to moderate growth, progressive, successful companies will have to look at gaining a foot-hold in new, non-traditional markets, like the emerging Hispanic-American market and African-American market. But as for appealing to and reaching these markets in the future, the future is now.

In almost as many areas as one can count, over-looked opportunities exist which could easily add millions to companies' bottom lines. And some key areas, for example are: restaurants (both fast-food and dine-in), automobile sales, financial services, athletic shoes and apparel, clothing, food and beverage products, cosmetics, electronics, tourism, utility companies even, and literally a whole host of other types of consumer-oriented products and services, including black haircare products.

The African-American market can bring wonderful fruit to creative entrepreneurs and managers who go after this market skillfully. For even in such unlikely markets as the black haircare industry, where retail sales are approximately $1 billion, according to the American Health and Beauty Aids Institute in Chicago, IL, roughly only one-third of that is spent with black-owned haircare companies. The other is spent often unknowingly with white-owned companies, who have set-up shop in this industry. One such white-owned company reportedly even exclusively trademarked the name "Africa" for all black haircare products, threatening to sue companies which dared to use the name Africa in their products, even if the company was black-owned.

In fact, since 1987, a full-scale battle has erupted in the ethnic haircare segment--one of the fastest growing in the health and beauty aids category.

This battle began when one of Revlon's executives made statements that questioned the future of black-owned businesses.

He stated in *Newsweek*, "In the next couple of years, black-owned businesses will disappear. They'll all be sold to white companies..." This set-off an eruption that can still be heard today. But nonetheless, unless black-owned companies get more aggressive in marketing and pricing products more competitively, beefing up their advertising budgets, training future young executives, and are able to acquire wider distribution channels, then unfortunately, Revlon's executive may be right. Just for your information, white-owned companies currently makeup more than 50% of the ethnic haircare market.

Quite frankly, the African-American market in the United States has been quietly growing in size and sheer economic strength for a number of years now. And blacks traditionally did not realize that due to the lack of corporate respect, their power was not in spending or buying merchandise, but is in their ability to *save and invest*. If many blacks become more conservative with their spending, and scale back often semi-luxurious life styles, then you would quickly realize Black America becoming an *Economic Powerhouse In the Light*.

Just take for example a company like Maybelline Cosmetics, a small company with its $400 million+ yearly revenues, in comparison to the cosmetic giants in which they have been up against like Revlon and Procter & Gamble's Cover Girl. They have been in an industry where gaining market share is just about impossible. But note what they did.

Growth slowed in Maybelline's $4 billion mass market cosmetics industry, and total units shipped grew just 3% in 1990. But in making specialized products for darker-skinned women, Maybelline saw a relatively untapped niche. "In the cosmetics business, everybody's been trying to fight it out on the same ground," said Robert Hiatt, Maybelline's chief executive officer. "What we found is that niches can be exploited."

What does this mean? It means that black women spend more than $600 million on makeup annually, and black consumers spend three times on average what white consumers do for cosmetics. On top of that, the population of blacks and frequently dark-skinned Hispanic-Americans, has been growing much faster than the population as a whole, and the number of blacks with annual household incomes above $35,000, rose more than 50% in the past decade. And just for your information, according to Maybelline, at least parts of its ethnic "Shades of You" line, is used by as many as 69% of African-American women. Also, according to Maybelline, their mascara is the number-one seller among black women (Sources: Maybelline Inc. & Forbes, June 24, 1991).

In the multi-billion dollar automobile market for instance, according to the *Wall Street Journal*, in 1994, blacks alone spent approximately $12 billion just on U.S. car and truck sales (includes both new and used vehicles).

But wait. Don't forget about the "small" African-American dollar. In many poor black neighborhoods, you will almost always seem to find a store or stores owned by Asians or persons from India. This is significant because these often high-dollar earning groups have shown that by not overlooking, but targeting the "small black dollar," unlike what many companies have done, one can become quite successful, and even become wealthy, with little or no bank loans, as many of these people have pooled their resources, and reaped the rewards.

Frankly, over the years, it seems that everyone has benefitted from the black consumer buying market and the dollars of blacks, but blacks. But as I have informed readers about the new age of more sophisticated, aggressive blacks which has emerged, many of whom are underemployed, sooner rather than later, you can expect for the above trend to make drastic changes. And just imagine how influential blacks would be if they began saving some of their earnings from vast purchases, deferred gratification, pooled, invested, and channeled their dollars in the same direction. Out of $300 billion, Black America would quickly become a force to be reckoned with--one that could be an ally, rather than hostile to those companies who have treated blacks with a lack of concern and disrespect.

Perhaps this truly is an opportunity for the politically astute, and financial services industry to begin cultivating this market, while it is still in its infancy stage. But more will definitely be discussed about this subject later in this text.

Getting The Record Straight

Though many blacks may have started out poor, many have not stayed that way, which is precisely what companies must understand if they are to continue to prosper in the future. However, one reason why many companies do not know or do not understand this already, is because many of today's rising blacks are "low-key" people. And unfortunately, the last thing the media often does is to show us these people, despite it's labeling of often being considered a "liberal body."

Obviously, we only see the side that appears more "newsworthy," like rapist, murderers, and the like--sensationalism, a far cry from the overall reality of black people.

It never ceases to amaze this author, that each time a bad incident appears on television, such as a robbery or other derogatory crime, if the person is black, almost always, his or her picture is shown. Often times, however, when perpetrators are white, their faces are rarely seen on television. Why is this?

There appears to also be an assault on rap and hip-hop music. For as a teen in Texas shot a Texas policeman, he said that he did it because he heard it talked about on a song released by rapper Tupac Shakur. Maybe, just maybe, this has merit. But wait. What about the numerous incidents of white teens smoking, doing drugs, Devil worshiping, and harming their parents, often because of Heavy Metal or Hard Rock? We hear about some of the heinous acts performed by these young people on a regular basis, and there often appears to be a direct link to these types of acts and the music listened to by these young persons, but the author has yet to see wide-spread media attention or otherwise, aimed at ending Heavy Metal or Hard Rock music. Are these not double standards?

You see, one reason for this often distorted, one-sided picture from the media, is that throughout various newsrooms across the country, editors of "mainstream" newspapers and magazines are almost all white, as well as the assignment editors for most television stations. Thus, the perception of Black America shown by these people, is often less complimentary, as stories are often shown from their perspectives, not necessarily the perspective of the group in which the story is being done.

Many editors and assignment editors have not experienced life from a black perspective, or any perspective other than white for that matter. And frankly, many of these people simply cannot identify well with the average black, because of the differences in everyday cultural and social experiences. This is why there are often calls to have the workplace look more like America really looks. This is also another reason why so many new discoveries in American History are just now being made as well. As it has long been considered in the black community, American History is simply, His-Story.

Candidly speaking, the arrogance posed by some in the media, which others would consider racist, ultimately hinders us all in this regard. Hence, you get black murderers and rapists shown on television, but hardly if ever, any black authors, artists and black literary coverage in your newspapers or on television.

And just for the record, with regard to where issues of crime and social problems exist, they are usually almost largely and directly attributed to and correlated with economics and finance.

In short, this is stated to conclude that Black Americans are not people with some type of inherent criminal nature, like some would perhaps have us to believe. But most people who are subjected to terrible economic conditions, and who can look around them to see extraordinary displays of wealth and extravagances, while they suffer, can easily be *at least tempted* to adopt a criminal mind-set.

Strip away our college educations, decent paying jobs, and give us poor, under-educated parents, and many of us would easily fall into such a category, which is no excuse, but it is reality. This is why the next ten years in our country, after our rich elite have been allowed to buy up everything, will be so interesting.

Briefly, let's look to Paris, France for a moment, a location noted for its traditional lack of crime and violence. Today in Paris, massive displays of wealth are off-set by areas with crime and violence so thick, the police are even afraid to enter certain areas. The reason? Because crime and violence has nothing to do with race. Instead, it has much to do with large disparities between economic classes. And though intellectually speaking, few would argue with this, privately, some still wonder. So, if you are one who has happened to fall into such a trap, then refer back to our discussion earlier in this chapter on groups believing that they are more different from other groups than they really are--the false pride and racism discussion.

Effectively Reaching African-Americans

Fortune 500's Take Notice

As late as 1994, it was surveyed that more than half of the Fortune 500 companies stated that they had some sort of ethnic marketing programs in place, aimed at reaching African-Americans. But as it may be a coincidence, I'll simply let you decide, most of the companies with less than progressive earnings lately, do not have ethnic marketing programs in existence. But regardless, marketing to African-Americans is not really a new thing, it's just that until recently, because of a lack of awareness, and in-depth knowledge about the market, it was just ignored. Although these attitudes are changing at those companies who are really interested in making money, many large opportunities exist for aggressive companies, large or small, who wish to grow.

Business Is Business

Ethnics already make-up approximately 25% of the total U.S. population; and in fact, ethnic minorities are majorities in one of every six U.S. cities, according to the U.S. Census Bureau. By the year 2002, non-white persons in the U.S. are expected to comprise one-third of the total U.S. population.

This is because many within the general market are choosing to have fewer children these days, many are unable to have children at all, and the increase in gay and lesbian couples are all helping to shape the drop in "general market" demographic growth rates. In all candor, this is a large reason why many whites have suddenly turned "conservative," and why White Supremacist groups are up in arms around the country.

Obviously, this data was a wake-up call for marketers when the 1990 Census report was released. And as many believe, the recent Republican sweep, and sudden popularity by former presidential candidate Pat Buchanan, is a last ditch effort by many white males to "reclaim America." If this is true, and I see no reason to doubt, then obviously, marketers weren't the only ones who noticed these changes.

In some of the nation's largest cities--New York, Washington, D.C., Atlanta..., more than half the residents are non-whites, and in some instances, as many as 70% of those populations are ethnic minorities. Even in many smaller metropolitan cities, minority populations are substantial, and could contribute *some real gains* to companies' bottom-line profit margins.

But all politics aside, in this case, business is business, and undoubtedly, ethnic marketing will fast prove itself as a choice business strategy of the future. So since this is likely to be the case, shouldn't your company be poised to take advantage of growth opportunities, changing markets, and the changing trends?

It should be reiterated right away, that marketing to today's, and tomorrow's ethnic markets, will be NO SIMPLE TASK. And of course, one must also understand the differences between the vehicles for effectively reaching these markets, versus just touching the surface too. Some of these vehicles are in many ways quite different from reaching general market audiences. One reason is because African-Americans are not like white consumers with darker skin. To market to blacks in this fashion is off-target to say the least.

And even though traditionally, black households have watched an average of about 50% more television per week than non-black households, again, black-owned agencies handle only about one-third of the amount marketers spend for advertising created to appeal to the African-American market.

And why is nearly $1 billion dollars spent to reach the black market in the first place? Because of black buying power! By a substantial margin, blacks are the nation's largest minority group, spending approximately $290 billion in 1994, compared with hispanics' $200 billion.

Just ask McDonalds if it is the number one hamburger chain in the world, and among African-Americans by accident. They will quickly tell you no, because quite frankly, by paying attention to market segments, McDonalds knows that blacks spend an enormous amount of money at drive-in restaurants, thus McDonald's profits have continued to pour-in as a result of their marketing efforts.

So, in order for African-Americans to really take notice of companies, and have their senses appealed to, black-owned agencies will undoubtedly have to handle much more than a mere one-third of black advertising and marketing business. McDonalds realizes this as it employs at least two black ad agencies. But other companies must also come to realize this fact as well, undoubtedly.

But having said that, please allow me to introduce you to two different common schools of thought believed by advertisers regarding this issue.

The General Market Agency School of Thought

Many large general market agencies are beginning to form special market divisions within their large structures, such as agencies like BBDO Worldwide, for instance.

Persons working within such divisions, many of whom are usually white, and have little in common with the black or hispanic people they are marketing to, often believe that they can tap ethnic markets just as good as anyone else, or at least, this is what they tell their clients. The reason these persons give is that good advertisers can advertise to anyone.

Well, while it may be true that good advertisers can get messages to anyone, the question is, are they the right messages, and have those messages been presented properly? Positioned in the proper mediums, and have other subtleties been considered?

It is estimated that more than half a billion dollars, or approximately 65% of the total amount spent on black-targeted advertising, is usually spent just converting general market ads to ethnic ads, by replacing white actors and models with black actors and models. A nameless American car company recently had a run-in with such a thing.

So as you may guess, in a nutshell, the majority of such efforts often fail, have disappointing returns on the investment, or backfire. These failed efforts can leave many companies left wondering if the ads they ran really lived up to their expectations? And this can obviously sometimes have a negative effect upon companies who have attempted to reach African-Americans, but were not very successful.

These misguided efforts often cause companies to question their better judgement, and thus miss-out on vast amounts of opportunities. Has your company ever done such things? If so, then I will give you a strong hint to the probable solution of such a problem--Take a good look at your ad agency.

If general market shops take a look, perhaps they will find some real opportunities by teaming-up with ethnic agencies, rather than attempting to do things that they are no good at. Some have already done this. However, I must warn that from this author's own experiences, as well as the experiences of other agencies whom the author has talked to, *I do not necessarily recommend this arrangement.* It has not seemed to work well for ethnic agencies. The reason is because usually, general market shops often try to learn the ethnic agency's expertise, then get rid of them. And undoubtedly, such predatorial relationships will not withstand the test of time, so fairness issues should be worked-out on the front end, if such joint ventures with larger firms are to be successful.

The Ethnic Marketing Agency School of Thought

Although marketing to African-Americans is what several successful companies have done, and what many undoubtedly will do, many companies still do not adequately utilize or recognize the need for why they should hire an ethnic advertising agency. I have had major billion dollar corporations as clients and potential clients, suggest to me, "We feel we do alright reaching blacks through our present general market advertisements. We're not sure that we need to target them separately, and even if we did, we're not convinced why we would need an ethnic ad agency to do it."

Now, as amazing as this may sound, I have heard this comment spoken time and time again, so let me address it this way... Aside from the obvious reasons why one would hire an ethnic ad agency to motivate ethnic audiences, when I stated earlier that today, and into the future, marketing to blacks is not and will not be simple, I was not even remotely kidding. And trying to wait to pursue this market could be one of the worst moves a company could make. This is because of the substantial brand loyalty and quality consciousness, among other things, which many African-Americans house--at least when black's senses are appealed to properly.

Half-hearted or patronizing efforts will no longer continue to stimulate the interest, nor the dollars of blacks. Today, blacks have become much more savvy. Many of today's and tomorrow's African-Americans will have to be aggressively sought-after with aggressive pull strategies, most likely by aggressive, skilled black agencies--entities which understand the intricacies of language, tastes, preferences, buying habits, sensitivity levels, etc., of today's African-Americans.

Let me give you a personal example. My agency once produced a couple of campaigns for a large out-of-state bank which was attempting to reach the black consumer market. The bank was solid, but had a public perception problem of only catering to old, white, and wealthy persons. With this challenge, we produced two solid campaigns. One of the ads featured a young black man and woman, who had just purchased a new car, with warm, emotional copy reading overhead. Now, my photographer was a white male, one who I consider to be fairly progressive with regard to race relations. He has a master's degree in photo journalism from a prestigious northeastern university, and is quite talented. However, while setting up the shot, he commented to me, "She's a pretty girl. Why don't we put her here (on the driver's side), and him there (on the passenger's side)..."

Now, many whites, even after visually seeing the ad, until the problem was pointed-out to them said, "What's wrong with that? Its a pretty ad, I like it!" However, many African-Americans would instantly pick up on what's wrong with that, right away. Although my photographer meant no harm, I mentioned to him, "What message would we be giving black males here...that they don't provide for their families, and can't buy a car, but their woman can?" This would have surely added fuel to the already down-trodden images of black males, no matter how well-intentioned the ad.

As this little matter was corrected, the ad was a success. However, this one campaign could have easily turned into a public relations nightmare, eliminating any progress which had already been made.

After finishing the ad, I ran the scenario by my clients at the bank. They too initially saw nothing wrong with this scenario, until I pointed-out the concern to them. After this, they immediately saw the ad from a different perspective, and told me that I was worth my weight in gold.

So, this is only to show that even though good advertisers perhaps can advertise to anyone, when marketing to ethnic markets without an ethnic agency, there are always important subtleties which can be missed or overlooked. Needless to say, these subtleties can go a long way in hindering progress or advancing progress for your company to appeal to, or gain the market share of ethnic customers.

But on another note, some ethnic agencies are frustrated that they often are only selected to work on minority-targeted advertising, or only produce creative. Their ethnic ads may be seen by mainstream audiences, but these agencies usually do not get the opportunity to serve as the lead agency for major advertisers, despite many being wonderfully creative, energetic, and multi-talented.

By getting general market business, this could mean that these agencies could receive bigger budgets, more exposure, and have more input on product marketing strategies, among other things.

But on the other hand, however, other ethnic agencies could care less about advertising to the general market. The reason is because the present general market, is a shrinking piece of pie.

Many ethnic advertisers know how to sell to whites, because that's how most got into the advertising business. However, in the future, many ethnic agencies see more explosive growth in niche marketing. For in the future, virtually everyone will have a niche. That's one of the reasons why many ethnic agencies began to specialize in ethnic marketing in the first place.

But one important note when marketing to the African-American consumer group--things do matter above and beyond simply what is seen and what is heard. It also very much matters how it is said, who says it, the perception to be involved...factors that quite frankly, only ethnic agencies can effectively handle for most clients.

Most organizations with profitable ethnic marketing programs in existence understand this, as they often have both an ethnic agency, and sometimes a general market agency also, such as Burger King, Chrysler, and McDonalds. Ironically, however, though often not utilized, many ethnic marketing firms are also able to skillfully perform the advertising function for both ethnic markets and the general market. This was realized when Mars Inc., the huge candy giant, hired New York ethnic agency Uniworld to handle its entire 3 Musketeers account for the United States. This was not the first of such developments, however.

Previously, again, with regard to Uniworld, Burger King did the same, allowing it to also handle their entire U.S. ad account, after firing its general market agency. The results? Sales increased sharply. But eventually, Uniworld took a back seat, as a white agency was again handed the general market business, while Uniworld was to concentrate only on ethnic markets.

But regardless, the reason for such diversity among many ethnic agencies, enabling them to perform remarkably in both ethnic markets and the general market, is that as it presently stands, most ethnic minorities have to be "bi-cultural," just in order to function "normally" in our society. So as such, many ethnic advertising professionals are able to effectively do both general market, and ethnic advertising and marketing. Why? Because today's advertising is usually "hip," and much of it is aimed at markets which are 25 and under. And as most "hipness" often comes from young black street culture, which then transcends into the mainstream, ethnic marketing often sets the pace for even the general market.

It should be noted that because many ethnic firms likely have only recently been "allowed" to compete in the same circles as long-time, well-established white firms, many still do not receive all of the opportunities they deserve, often times surviving off of project work, and not being allowed to place media. As such, many of these firms obviously may not have as long of a track record as their counterparts, but does not mean that they are any less effective.

So, keep this in mind when weighing the criteria for competing agencies. For, by placing too much emphasis on firm size, years in business, etc., other important factors could be overlooked, like smart, savvy, creative, intelligent and *effective* advertising, which doesn't always come from old, established firms all of the time.

Today is quickly proving that huge agencies on Madison Avenue no longer have monopolies on good creative advertising. For with new, changing technology, some of the smaller shops are now able to compete, and some have already run rings around some of the big guys. After all, in many ways, technology has now put these groups on a level playing field.

If your goal is to bring-in vast amounts of profitable black business, then that goal will likely only reasonably be brought to full, long-term fruition by an advertiser who is creative, knowledgeable, and skilled in various areas related to African-American targeted advertising, marketing, public relations and research. This should not be entrusted to an agency who sees this area as one to be exploited, and therefore simply adds such a service onto its services offered column. Unfortunately and pathetically, this has begun to happen at some general market agencies, smelling an "exploitable niche." Some of these firms seek to go head-to-head with ethnic marketers, attempting to put them out-of-business, even if their firms have few or no ethnic marketers on their large staffs. This is not optimally beneficial to clients seeking to really make an impact in ethnic markets.

So, the thought of reaching specific ethnic markets, without a skilled ethnic agency, is not wise, the ethnic agency group will tell you. For utilizing a general market agency, usually staffed full of affluent whites, to reach blacks, hispanics, and other racial minorities, is as noted ethnic advertising veteran Tom Burrell put it, "like the equivalent of hiring a doctor who's a general practitioner to perform brain surgery."

No Longer Just A Secondary Market

As the African-American market was once seen as merely a secondary market by many general market ad agencies, for many companies, it is now an integral part of the overall advertising and marketing planning process.

Various relevant elements and attitudes exist which often cannot be properly identifiable by an "outside source." These include political views, cultural experiences, social experiences, socio-economics, the works. Research is also an exceptional reason why companies should call upon skilled ethnic firms. This is so as blacks are often more likely to have unlisted telephone numbers, and be less cooperative with white researchers trying to get information from them. So, in such situations, without ethnic firms, companies can encounter severe problems, and this should be so noted.

Such issues often handicap white agencies from being able to do the best job for their clients, and often, when they try, they are just getting costly training at their client's expense. These things often make general market agencies bring in lack-luster results, and it is still difficult to imagine why a company would seek to reach ethnic markets without a skilled, ethnic agency. It just makes good common sense, doesn't it? But regardless, and quite frankly, when a company is seeking real results, in most instances, it likely would be better-off by hiring a talented ethnic agency to reach minority consumers. After all, the face of the marketplace is changing, thus shouldn't the advertisers change some too? Just weigh that for what it's worth.

Arming The Advertiser

Please note that in order to accomplish whatever a company's goals and objectives might be, companies must arm the advertiser responsible for minority-targeted marketing, whomever the agency, with a budget feasible enough to "pull" and motivate African-Americans to buy particular products.

Although this may appear obvious, relating back to some of my own experiences, I have also often encountered large companies, who wished for my agency to assist them in tapping into ethnic markets, but with budgets far less than what would be satisfactory to do so. In fact, one example of many, is when a billion dollar nameless company, with a million dollar ad budget, and a sizeable black population as its target, wanted me to plan a year-long African-American targeted campaign with an $18,000 budget, media included. They emphasized that they wanted real results. When I almost choked, I was asked what was wrong, was the budget too low? I thought, "And you have to ask?" So as such, time-out. This requires some discussion.

Those of you familiar with the costs of advertising can understand why I nearly choked. Though I should be accustomed to such discussions by now, I will probably never really get used to them. But anyhow, for those who do not understand, this situation is a travesty. A budget is an extremely important factor, and to cut it because you will be marketing to African-Americans will likely be a big mistake, as was learned by most organizations within my own experiences. Many today, however, have seen the light, and are scrambling to play catch-up, but unfortunately, they are still the minority, so don't start the celebrations just yet. And I am also reminded of the dozens of small business owners who have asked me, "I have $300, what can you do with that?" I usually politely reply "nothing," so I often end up simply donating services in this regard.

As I advised people then, I advise people today, be very careful so you do not conduct your ethnic marketing programs in a patronizing or half-hearted manner. For if you do, be forewarned that you will likely only see half-hearted or patronizing returns. I cannot overstate that today's better-educated, aggressive, savvy African-Americans can prove to be a tough nut to crack and convince. So, if commitment, both financially, emotionally, etc., is not an integral part of an organization's marketing efforts, then I would strongly advise that organization not to waste its time or money, because likely, that will be all it would be doing.

To sum it all up, I will repeat to you what I once heard a seasoned ad man years ago tell one of his clients. I believe he borrowed this phrase from the noted advertising professional, J. Walter Thompson, founder of one of the largest general market advertising agencies in the world. He stated, "Advertising is like flying an airplane, if you do not supply it with enough fuel, the plane will surely go down before it reaches its destination, such is the case with advertising." In short, advertising must be equipped with enough "fuel" to effectively saturate the target market, or it will fall short virtually every time--this fuel is your budget.

Another point to make, however, is that while companies can compare budgets with approximate budgets of other companies in their respective industries, note that your company may still need to overcome emotional or perceptive obstacles that other organizations may have already surpassed, or begun to surpass years ago. So in essence, as your organization may be currently positioned, it may likely need to play catch up, so evaluate this factor accordingly.

Also, companies should be warned henceforth that the benefits of an ethnic marketing program will not come overnight, as with anything else in life usually worth obtaining. It may take several months, or even years to fully realize the maximum potential associated with this market. So, if an organization has been stubborn in this regard in years past, it should be ready to pay the piper, as it may have to be just a little bit patient when expecting overnight results.

Differences In Language, Tastes, Preferences and Perception

While it is true that most general market advertising is seen by most African-Americans, most African-Americans usually are not motivated or affected by such messages. For with any group of people, companies will almost always receive much better results when they do not use a "shotgun" approach, but rather use a tailored message to reach a particular audience. But the bottom line consideration is that the average black and white, at the risk of sounding stereotypical, display profound differences in language, tastes, preferences and perception. These things can have a significant impact, especially when attempting to stimulate the interests and dollars of African-Americans.

But for right now, it should also be noted that organizations and entities which target African-Americans, will likely be rewarded richly, if they allow African-Americans to express their own identity, and treat black's concerns with respect.

For example, StoveTop Stuffing discovered that language can affect the way African-Americans perceive products, as blacks usually refer to this type of food as "dressing," not "stuffing." When StoveTop noticed this difference, it began targeting blacks with a commercial that uses the word "dressing" instead of "stuffing," sales improved. Now, while a general market agency can produce a good commercial, an ethnic agency will likely also be able to pick up on the little, but subtle, important details like this. As with any true art, the mastery is in the details. So before millions of dollars are wasted on airing the wrong message, I advise that you hire an ethnic ad agency.

Music is another important means of communication sometimes overlooked by general market advertisers, as a few years ago, the Greyhound Bus Company decided to reach-out to blacks by running commercials on black radio stations. But instead of tailoring its message to black consumers, the company aired the same general market spot that was aired on other radio stations. The problem? These commercials had a country-western soundtrack, which is the least favored music genre among blacks, so what do you think was likely the outcome?

While it is impossible to say whether Greyhound actually lost any black customers because of this commercial or not, it is likely a safe bet to say that they didn't attract as many blacks as they would have with tasteful, contemporary urban music. But just for your information, Greyhound later unveiled a new commercial which uses black talent--not necessarily, but likely the result of efforts by an ethnic agency.

As far as perception goes, many factors often influence how blacks and whites perceive certain things, but of course, you know that by now. Taking a look at the O.J. Simpson trial for a moment, as you'll recall, most whites perceived that O.J. was guilty versus many blacks perceiving that O.J. was not guilty, or at least, that there wasn't sufficient evidence to over-ride a perjured, racist cop, to convict beyond a reasonable doubt. But nonetheless, another poll was also conducted concerning who was the most astute attorney in the courtroom. What do you think was the outcome? Most whites said the lead prosecutor, Marcia Clark (white), while most blacks favored O.J.'s lead, Johnny Cochran (black)--as with any group, perception is reality.

Beyond Just Black And White

Before we get off on a tangent of just black and white, however, it should be clearly noted that many differences are just as big a part of the marketing process as black and white. Many call these differences "psychographics."

You see, to make a long story short, for anyone to be able to clearly understand a market, one must also understand the problems and obstacles faced by that market. This is at the real core of psychographic, buyer behavior analysis. So, as we move forward, a person would do him or herself a favor by paying particular attention to the causes of the effects.

Today, with the increasing numbers of black journalists, television producers, writers and directors, actors, professional athletes, musicians, advertising agency owners, doctors, lawyers, politicians, and a whole host of other black professionals, one can much more easily realize that a substantial number of blacks are considered affluent, or at least middle class. And again, "affluent" loosely means blacks earning approximately $50,000+ household incomes.

As such, many blacks also now live in the suburbs, which incidentally, a recent study showed that blacks, on the average, pay higher property taxes when living in suburban areas than do whites. But nonetheless, the numbers of blacks who have moved to the suburbs has grown substantially. Many of today's African-Americans do virtually the same things that once traditionally whites only performed, such as play golf, tennis, etc. So quite simply, there is no longer necessarily a simple, clear distinction between blacks and whites in the area of consumer purchases, and for those who are astute enough, some large opportunities exist as such. Does all of this confuse the issue between simply who is black and who is white? You bet your socks it does.

Companies today must pay much closer attention to exactly who their markets are. Historically, most blacks did one particular thing, while most whites usually did the opposite, but that is no longer necessarily the case. Today, blacks purchase golf clubs and equipment, tennis paraphernalia, suburban housing, stocks, bonds, other financial services, books, and literally a whole host of other products traditionally thought to only be purchased by whites only, or at least with there being no significant black purchases. And again, these purchases are so, as many times, there is still a significant income disparity between blacks and whites. But this is not to say that some things aren't still like the old days, because unfortunately, some are.

Today, there is likely to be just as great a difference between an inner-city, urban black youth, and an average, forty year-old, black suburban professional, as it is for a black youth and the average suburban white person. Today, younger blacks and most older blacks are at two different ends of the spectrum when it comes to evaluating their views, perceptions, and tastes. Often times, these things might be significantly different, causing the need for even greater understanding when segmenting and communicating to today's African-American audience.

This is but one example of many, when for one reason or another, blacks and whites of different ages, backgrounds, etc., have profoundly different perceptions about certain messages, events, and the like.

Environmental surroundings and experiences are often the main reasons for differences between people, which might explain why many blacks and whites can see the exact same messages, and still draw two distinctly different conclusions about what they just saw. This thereby makes the discussions after the O.J. Simpson trial, of jurors being required to have certain levels of education, and the like, virtually preposterous. Why this is hardly any different from making citizens pay poll taxes.

Does General Market Advertising Work On Minorities?

We've all seen the infamous one minority in a sea of white faces ads. So undoubtedly, some general market advertising does have an effect on racial minorities, but in most cases, is it a positive effect, and/or does it have more than a limited effect?

One should be cautioned that running a single ad, broadcast spot or the like, usually will not draw the desired responses one might be looking for. Multiple marketing efforts will be required, with the investment being for the long-term. It should also be added that an educated corporate staff, and community buy-in is essential, which again, takes commitment, and must be non-patronizing.

But having said all of that, the lack of competition in this market is almost amazing, considering the size and sheer value of such a market. This creates vast numbers of golden opportunities for entrepreneurs and companies, big or small.

However, the fact that businesses have been somewhat slow and awkward in their approach to market to African-Americans is likely costing a number of companies untold fortunes. This is because whoever thinks enough of African-Americans to meaningfully reach-out to blacks first, will likely solidify a large chunk of market share, which can have considerable brand loyalty, and a whole host of other favorable factors, *if appealed to properly.*

But obtaining success in this market ultimately will depend upon prompt action, coupled with the ability to recognize the differences among ethnic groups. With the changing times, companies will have little choice but to immediately create programs that appeal to the individual wants and needs of specific ethnic groups, or face being left behind.

Benefits When Marketing To African-Americans

African-Americans are generally loyal to those entities, groups or organizations who reach out to blacks, and are not driven by racism, greed or prejudice. This is largely why so many corporations around the country began to sponsor African-American activities and promotions, and have engaged in more ethnic promotions types of activities, than ever before.

Specific benefits which can be expected as a result of properly marketing to African-Americans and stimulating their interests are:

- Product/Customer Loyalty.

- Spending exceeding general market spending patterns.

- Receptivity.

- A handsome return on advertising, marketing & promotions investments.

- More "recession proof" than traditional markets.

- African-Americans are loyal patrons to those who put forth the effort and necessary resources to make them feel welcome and respected by an organization.

- African-Americans are among one of the fastest growing segments of the population.

- African-Americans are the largest ethnic minority group in the country.

- African-Americans are one of the largest consumer groups in the country, and are the largest consumer group in many product classifications.

A whole host of other secondary favorable outcomes exist, but quite frankly, without a doubt, the African-American market segment is hands-down, a clear and decisive choice for the continued survival/advancement of many companies of the future, big or small.

And when organizations consider that their bread and butter customers are really $20,000 per year ethnic wage-earning customers, then marketing will begin to take on whole new forms, shapes and dimensions.

But whether we admit it, or even realize it, African-Americans virtually keep our economy moving with their purchases, even during recessions. So as blacks can be viewed as somewhat recession-proof, shopping even during rough economic times, more so than the average American, then this would certainly create a benefit for entrepreneurs, companies and marketers. This makes African-Americans a more stable, and perhaps less cyclical, almost "recession proof" market, more so than anyone else. But this also assumes of course, that African-Americans continue to break glass ceilings, and are not kept from earning high incomes through devious legislation measures, bitter envy, etcetera.

Helpful Hint

Likely, some of the best and most dedicated advertising and marketing work will come from smart, small, aggressive advertising and marketing agencies, because many are hungry, have less overhead, and will be more competitively priced. Also, surprisingly, those shops with well-trained professionals with diversified skills, often will give companies exactly what they've been looking for, while wasting less of a client's money on agency overhead.

Although not all of them are listed in the Standard Directory of Advertisers, make no mistake about it, aggressive, lean and mean ethnic agencies are available, and more are popping up everyday to help entrepreneurs and companies build value for their organizations.

Ethnic Marketing Is Mainstream Marketing

Questioning Our Rationale

According to the U.S. Census Bureau, statistically speaking, the hispanic demo-graphic segment has been the second fastest growing demographic group (grew by 53% between 1980-1990), while Asians reside as number one (grew by nearly 108% during the same time period). This can be somewhat misleading, however, as often times, much attention often too hastily shifts away from the African-American market segment, somehow, when talking about ethnic marketing.

The wisdom of such shifts should certainly be questioned, as presently, the African-American segment has the largest minority population in the country, numbering roughly 30 million persons, or 12% of the U.S. population. Hispanics number approximately 22 million persons, or 9% of the

U.S., and unfortunately, many are illegal immigrants, due to overcrowding and lack of opportunities in Mexico. Asians number 7 million, or roughly only 3% of the U.S. population, according to the census bureau.

Now, a point to consider, is that even though the Asian population is growing in the U.S., from a marketing perspective, separate marketing initiatives are often viewed as not necessary. The reasons are three-fold. Number one, Asians, while perhaps growing in statistical significance, are still a much smaller minority group than blacks or hispanics. Number two, Asians are tracked very broadly by the census bureau, which means any number of groups with different cultures, may likely be counted as Asians, making proper segmentation very difficult (i.e. Chinese, Japanese, Vietnamese, Koreans, Taiwanese, Filipinos, etc.). Number three, many more Asians often assimilate into mainstream culture than most other ethnic groups.

In other words, most Asians often act, think, respond, and perceive things in roughly the same way as do most whites. Many Asians around the country live in mostly suburban neighborhoods, many vote Republican, they often go to the same schools as whites, and act in many other ways as most suburban whites. This creates almost a lack of need for any real, specialized, targeted promotions and advertising, when targeting most Asian-Americans.

Today, hispanics are growing rapidly, but in the meanwhile, blacks still reside as America's largest minority group. And blacks by far have the largest middle-class among minority groups, and still have a significantly higher than general market growth rate. Marketers often recognize the differences between the "general market" and the hispanic market, because of the obvious language barrier. But in reaching African-Americans, many companies still have not gotten the picture. Many companies still do not recognize the $300 billion black buying market, and when they do, these companies attempt to reach this group primarily, or exclusively through general market advertising. This usually just doesn't work.

The bottom line--companies must understand what marketing means when targeting blacks. And the lack of knowledge about this market, creates a scenario where its real potential is still yet to be realized.

Blacks And Education

Because of socio-economics, and American history, people often formulate opinions about other people, namely blacks, which do not necessarily "look like us." It has been assumed that hispanics are lazy, women on jobs will have to take a lot of time off to raise children, and blacks are poor, uneducated, and unqualified. So, let's take a look at the realities, compared to the perceptions.

As of 1995, according to the U.S. Bureau of Labor Statistics, there were more than 2.7 million blacks who were college graduates. This number is more than one-third of every man, woman and child, who is Asian-American. Translated another way, this number would be the same as meaning that every single American Indian and Eskimo in the United States has a college degree, and there would still be more blacks with degrees remaining. In fact, there was more than a 43% increase in the number of blacks with college degrees in the past decade.

So, these statistics obviously run contrary to the perceptions about blacks being qualified, and their educations. But as some Americans would rather spend their time seeking to repudiate these and such figures, rather than simply acknowledging that they have allowed prejudiced attitudes to overtake their better judgement, this undoubtedly has also caused many companies to lose-out on yet another one of God's great blessings, and perhaps untold fortunes as well. Let's take a look to see what I mean.

More Than A Little Bit Mainstream

Although people marvel at them, often times, people never wonder where many consumer-oriented items that we so love today ever came from. And as consumers, perhaps that's fine. But as business persons, maybe we should take a closer look as you will see.

African-Americans are more creative and visionary than people often give blacks credit for being. So, let's ponder for a moment, the "mainstream" things in which blacks have created, often times with little or no formal educations even, while generating fortunes in business revenues. As you may know, African-Americans invented things such as: the kitchen table, mobile refrigeration system, traffic light, folding bed, rotary engine, ironing board, gas mask, lawn mower, fire extinguisher, elevator, mop, clothes drier, horse shoe, golf-tee, printing press, pencil sharpener, machine for forming vehicles, peanut butter, filament for light bulbs, telephone transmitter, and rapid fire gun (machine gun), just to name a few (Source: U.S. Patent Office).

Now, just think if you could have cornered the market on any of these products before they became "mainstream." That's right, you would be as many people became, very, very rich. However, few of these people were black, for white men often took these products, as blacks were in a position to be exploited. But nonetheless, the above is just a very, very partial list of many, upon many African-American developed products/inventions, which have become more than just a little bit mainstream.

Now my point here is that often times, blacks, whether blacks even realize it or not, are to a large degree, trend-setters. Young American culture, no matter what ethnicity the individual, is essentially driven by African-American street culture. And whether we realize it or not, this is not a trend that will likely stop anytime soon. In fact, this has been the case for decades.

In the early 1980's, as one example, there became an exceptional amount of attention being paid to athletes, and the apparel they wore by young, urban blacks. And as a result, even though it may have been tough on the pocket books, many of these people bought the sneakers, tee-shirts, warm-ups..., wore them to school, and thus a nation-wide fashion trend emerged. Hence, this type of marketing, which began appealing to black, urban youths, once again exploded into mainstream culture, and the results simply speak for themselves.

As a matter of fact, after observing in one poor, largely black neighborhood, I couldn't help but notice that every youngster outside had on a pair of Nikes or wore Nike apparel. No wonder why Nike recently reported proud quarterly earnings of more than $150 million. However, at the same time, it is reported that Nike has very few African-Americans in key decision-making positions. Also, one additional point which you might find interesting, is Nike's advertisements.

Notice that Nike, nor its competitor's advertisements rarely talk about the features and benefits of their shoes. Rather, they heavily rely on the use of big name, mostly black athletes, and their action on the basketball court, football field, track, or whatever, to sell their shoes, instead. What should this tell us?

My point here is that ethnic marketing often times evolves into mainstream marketing, or perhaps more appropriately, creates mainstream demand for products--Just ask successful companies like Coca-Cola for instance, where diversity has been much more than just a theory over the last few years. Why do you think Coke has run so many ads with African-Americans portrayed in them? What do you think they know that you don't? If you've been paying attention to the pages of this book, you might have a really good idea.

Quite simply, African-Americans are leading-edge trend-setters, pace-makers, whatever you want to call them. And ultimately, since African-Americans are such large consumers who are quality conscious, then often times, what they buy into is what ultimately sells to us all, blacks, whites, latinos, whoever.

Rock-n-roll, rap, jazz, rhythm and blues, catchy phrases and hip-hop, are just some of the many more recent commercialized success stories created by African-Americans, which were later brought into "mainstream culture" with astonishing success. And make no mistake about it, many of tomorrow's successes lie within the African-American market too.

Remember Vanilla Ice, the young white kid turned rapper? Although young black youths had been rapping for years in the inner cities, with little attention being paid to them, once Vanilla Ice came onto the scene, America loved him, and I'm talking "mainstream" America. Suddenly, he, unlike his predecessors, was appearing on morning news shows, late night television, and all of the above. In fact, just go into any apparel store, and be surprised if you don't see racks of clothes being marketed as hip-hop fashions. And of course, you wonder where hip-hop came from, right? You guessed it, African-Americans.

My ultimate point simply is that any company which overlooks African-Americans, and what blacks have to offer, is doing itself a grave injustice, whether they're targeting African-Americans as employees, vendors, customers, or both. And if these companies do not try to reach blacks soon, many certainly will be playing catch up, and will likely unsuccessfully try to reach blacks later.

Frankly, if prejudices do not interfere with the better business judgement decision of marketing to blacks, then many businesses could profit more than just a little bit.

Underestimating

Ever heard of Cecil Rhodes, the wealthy British industrialist in which the prestigious Rhodes Scholarship was named after? Well, in a nutshell, he resided in a place once named after him in South Africa, called Rhodesia? Today, that city is the modern day city of Zimbabwe. Anyway, here's the story.

Cecil Rhodes went to Africa approximately one century ago. He found beautiful land in which he decided to carve out thousands of acres for himself, conveniently rich with diamonds and gold. But he also found great architecture, which he allegedly believed to be the Lost City of the Queen of Sheba. Rhodes alleged that this could have therefore meant that it was from a lost tribe of whites.

Regardless to whether Zimbabwe was the Lost City, and it was proven later that it was not, Rhodes, a racist, attempted to undermine the claim of African nationalists to the right of the land, by laying claim to it, and ultimately robbing the native land of its rich resources. Historians debate over whether Rhodes did this for the betterment of Great Britain, for his own personal gain, or both, but having collected billions in gold and diamond revenues, what do you think?

Nonetheless, however, the beauty in which Rhodes saw, and the rich architecture that he realized, made him think that blacks could not have possibly produced such magnificent works. So in his mind, allegedly, the things in which he saw could not have been created by blacks, as they were too magnificent, he thought. He was wrong.

The moral to this story is that we today, are still falling into such traps without realizing the potential genius of people who others often tend to overlook or try to discredit. Isn't it odd that the group which has been cited as the first inhabitants of the Earth, appears to be the last to gain respect?

Minority Marketing As An Investment

As it is usually the goal of any manager or business owner to responsibly maximize profits, then the act of wisely and prudently marketing to African-Americans, will almost certainly more than justify the investment with handsome, profitable rewards.

As with anything, minority marketing being no exception, one gets out of something no more than what one puts in, and a less than aggressive ethnic marketing investment at this "near late-breaking" point, can prove very costly to your company later-on, in terms of your organization giving up in opportunity costs, what it could have had. Such mistakes, and missed opportunities, could easily cause a company to quickly be left behind, wondering where it went wrong?

Companies of the future should be cautious of the continuing practice of sinking vast dollars into general market campaigns/strategies in which the return rate on the investment will continue to be flat or soon decline. What I am telling you is that today, in most instances, when you market to the African-American market, you will hence be marketing to the general market.

In a nutshell, what I am telling you is that it is likely that a company would benefit greatly by planning for the future--take notice of the changing trends, demographics, flat general market growth rates, and invest where the growth will be, and often where the trends will be--ethnic markets, and more specifically, the African-American market.

So, to wrap things up, the African-American market is one market that I would definitely advise people not to overlook, and a market which I would advise companies and individuals to put their money on.

Within a few short years, if companies show a continuing commitment to the tastes and interests of African-Americans, then their gains/marketing in-flow dollars will likely rival those of the present general market, if not surpass the general market. Such activities will likely reward companies with a much higher than average rate-of-return on their investments, dollar for dollar.

What Marketing To Blacks Means To Tourism

To give you one example of an entire industry, which has until recently, ignored such an economic force, take the tourism industry for example. Including everything from hotels and motels, to restaurants, it was only discovered within the past few years that African-Americans actually spend more than $25 billion on domestic tourism alone in our country, not including conventions! And with a market so rich in rewards, to this day, very little competition still actively competes for black dollars, which could easily place a lagging city or state at the tourism forefront. It is virtually an untapped market. But instead, however, many locations have still continued to wage battle in the general market, a market that is vastly over-saturated with competition, and is declining sharply, demographically.

While compiling research, I visited the cities of Montgomery, Alabama and Atlanta, Georgia, two notable civil rights locations. While at these locations, one could only notice a warm spirit and atmosphere which appeared to circulate on the part of both blacks and whites. But whether this is actually still the case or not, who can say, however, the point is that until recent events of chain-gangs surfaced in Alabama, and some disturbing racial activity in Atlanta, over all, having racially hospitable locations has been very good for business.

Despite the heart-wrenching tragedies over the issues of civil and human rights, both cities appear to be moving along quite progressively, blacks and whites together--and business is thriving. But recently, some have wished to bring such progress to an end, as some have been aroused with envy. As you know, the 1996 Olympics was hosted in Atlanta, and Alabama even shared, with the city of Birmingham hosting at least one of these events. Undoubtedly, the apparent cohesiveness, and progress of these cities is a large factor why they were chosen. And by the way, for your information, both cities just happen to have black mayors.

In this author's opinion, these types of favorable attitudes are extremely important to any city, state, organization, or entity, which expects to successfully advance to levels of greatness and high profitability. While this is true when marketing to anyone, it's especially true with today's African-Americans.

Enterprisingly enough, both Georgia and Alabama have turned once tragedies of our nation's past into thriving profit centers. In the cities of Birmingham and Montgomery for instance, these were once places that were shameful, but have recently emerged as symbols of progress, and sources of great tourist revenues associated with ethnic marketing.

In Birmingham, the National Civil Rights Memorial resides, and has become one of the state's largest tourist attractions. In 1991, more than 200,000 people visited the site. The memorial was designed by Maya Lin, the architect who also designed the Vietnam War Memorial in Washington, D.C. And like the Vietnam Memorial, it has a strong effect on visitors.

In the city of Montgomery alone, tourists spend approximately $300 million per year, and a significant number of the city's tourists are black. Alabama has been courting African-American tourists since 1983, when state officials published a brochure highlighting black heritage attractions. And to date, more than 100,000 booklets have been sent across the nation, due to some diligent and hard work by the tourism folks in Alabama. These types of results are only an example to show that if invited, African-Americans will come.

In the City of Montgomery, at the time of my visit, approximately 3 buses arrived at its memorial each day, and each bus carried between 38 and 43 overnight visitors who leave behind about $5,000 in tourist spending. No data is available on the race of memorial visitors, but with an estimated return of $25 for every $1 invested in promotions, the only color local businesses care about is green!

African-Americans are far less likely than whites to go camping or hunting, and are less likely to engage in adventurous or risky activities like bungee jumping. They are, however, interested in attractions relevant to them like shopping, dining and

night-life. But travel per se can be difficult for African-Americans, and must be realized by industry persons or entrepreneurs wishing to get into the industry.

African-Americans are sometimes asked to carry bags, park cars, and take restaurant orders by others who assume they are employees. Flight attendants sometimes assume that blacks don't belong in the first-class section of airplanes, so black travelers are sometimes confronted when trying to store items in first-class closets and bins. All of these types of instances are obviously unacceptable if attempting to stimulate a company's economic growth by targeting ethnic markets.

Black Consumer Power

No matter what type of business you might be in, a lot can happen when a company or organization does not proactively, and effectively address the concerns of black consumers. Let's take a look at what happened in one such instance.

In 1990, in the city of Miami, FL, the black community declared a nation-wide economic boycott against Miami's $7 billion tourism industry. Ending the agreement took 16 months to negotiate, and in the process, the boycott cost an estimated $50 million in lost revenues--primarily the result of lost *black business*--conventions, conferences, etc.

The agreement which ended the boycott, called upon Miami's business community to commit to black economic empowerment by providing loans, bonding, insurance and private contracting opportunities for black businesses--things many blacks believe should have been made available a long time ago. Commitments for scholarships, internships, job training and financial aid for black students seeking careers in the multi-billion dollar Miami tourism industry, were also part of the agreement.

A $250,000 donation for 125 scholarships to train black students, and a deposit of $2.5 million into Florida's only black-owned bank, were also among other initiatives.

The boycott began shortly after the City of Miami, and five Cuban-American mayors, refused to officially welcome then anti-apartheid leader, and today, South African President, Nelson Mandela, during his visit to the city. The boycott quickly began to tarnish Miami's image around the world, for people began to see it as a sign of a divided community. The boycott demonstrated that African-Americans have an enormous economic impact on the tourism industry. And according to some reports, says the *Miami Herald*, the city went almost one year without booking a single convention.

After such a boycott, *some* are beginning to finally take blacks more seriously, and many have become more sensitive to the aspirations and frustrations of African-Americans. However, sadly enough, many more of these and such instances will likely have to take place before companies really get the message.

The lesson here? When companies and organizations don't perform adequately, or do not treat black's concerns with respect, they may find-out that today's blacks, however grudgingly, will use their economic clout, which can have a strong effect on virtually any organization economically. And today, unlike the past, blacks are much more likely to finally use that clout, especially against large, exploitative entities.

A Start To Attracting Profits From African-Americans

For those companies who market to African-American customers, respect and acceptance will continue to be paramount issues. And in attracting African-American patrons in the first place, companies undoubtedly will have to make a special effort at reaching this market. But as with any solid business initiative, companies should likely first evaluate the market for its specific products. Hire a professional or professionals who know that market, then begin with a *reasonable* investment, gauge your progress, make any changes accordingly, and go for it. If your efforts haven't been making steady progress, then re-evaluate your company's efforts and attitudes, revise accordingly, and re-initiate.

The *Wall Street Journal* noted in one of its articles, "African-Americans have more money to spend, are far more avid shoppers, and are far more brand-loyal and more receptive than most markets realize...But, marketers and advertisers have a long way to go in reaching African-Americans effectively."

This article hit the situation right on the head. The continued reluctance on the part of companies to aggressively move forward to attract this market will be a disaster for many companies in the future. Research indicates that African-Americans can, and can being the operative word, be far more brand-loyal than many other demographic groups. This means that a company which can captivate and stimulate the interest of blacks in a particular market, may likely come away as a big winner, being a leader in a market, which again, has little fierce competition, and big bucks to be gained as a result.

It is also equally important to note that to successfully market to African-Americans, a great deal of effort and commitment will be required-- from a budgetary standpoint, and personal commitment on the part of company executives, marketers, and frontline employees. But just remember that ethnic marketing programs are no different from making any other great investment--invest for the long-term, and allow time for growth before seeking to reap any real rewards.

In all fairness to you, so that companies may do it right, I must again tell you that I sincerely believe that it is not only smart, but imperative that an ethnic agency be charged with the ethnic marketing and advertising functions, for a number of reasons such as:

1) To appeal to or motivate. Copy likely should address African-American related designs/messages, that frankly, can only be properly handled by an African-American agency.

2) The proper levels of sensitivity must be used when marketing to African-Americans, for efforts viewed as patronizing, etc., can have effects far worse than never marketing to African-Americans at all, which would too be a big mistake.

3) Extensive interaction may be required with members throughout various African-American communities, and to obtain the best results, satisfaction and interpretation of African-Americans' wants, needs and desires, those things should be effectively addressed by a capable ethnic ad agency.

4) African-Americans' language, tastes, and preferences-- words, pictures, music selections, etc. that offend or do not motivate African-Americans, likely cannot be *effectively* addressed without an ethnic agency.

5) It could be an embarrassment, and later a public relations nightmare, for a company to appear non-exploitative when it is marketing to African-Americans, but does so without even using an ethnic agency. Negative vibes could certainly be sent as a result, which can certainly affect the outcome or impact of public relations or marketing initiatives. In other words, a company could be caught in the rain without an umbrella.

What Is Recommended
When Marketing To African-Americans

Because of the further fragmentation of communications mediums, it is suggested that a combination of both direct messages aimed specifically at African-Americans, and general audience messages be combined to attract African-American customers.

It is imperative that general audience messages show a much greater presence of African-Americans doing things that African-Americans do, where they do them. For when African-Americans see advertisements with little African-American representation, or messages with blacks appearing out-of-place, that message will reiterate that "This company has little interest in, nor respect for blacks, only our dollars." This will thus turn away African-American customers, and result in millions in lost profits.

The messages in both general audience advertisements and direct minority-aimed advertisements must be consistent in showing that African-Americans are just as much an integral part of a company's customers as any other group. This of course, if that is really the case, which it is with most common products. But nonetheless, inconsistent messages can thwart any further attempts to reach blacks, which would not be good.

Also, service-oriented companies should seek to make their products more tangible--people, blacks especially, often react to what can be seen, touched, heard, or felt, unlike most services.

Quite clearly, as we prepare to go into the 21st Century, it cannot be overstated that African-Americans are as savvy a group of consumers as any other. This is also coupled with the fact that many blacks are beginning to recognize that most businesses are targeting their 30 million person segment because of their yearly buying power, and nothing less.

So, this translates into an environment of where actions must speak louder than words when marketing to today's group of African-Americans, but nonetheless, an environment where words do count.

WHAT EVERY AMERICAN

SHOULD KNOW...

In the previous chapters, you have been informed about the myriad of reasons why the African-American market should be considered for business opportunities. And by now, perhaps you have become convinced. If not, then perhaps all of the intellectual discussions in the world will be of little use. But regardless, we're now about to change gears.

You're probably tired of discussing it, and I'm sure you've heard much of the debate about it, but regardless, affirmative action cannot be overlooked as a viable key to Black America's existence as an *Economic Powerhouse In The Dark*. As such, it must be addressed in this chapter.

So, in taking a holistic approach, and as it is paramount that one clearly understand all which surrounds this issue, we will address it candidly and openly in this chapter.

Why Many Wonder

Despite the common thoughts of many, some of the first early blacks to come to America were not slaves. Many black "immigrants" came initially as did many European immigrants, bound as indentured servants for a number of years, then freed. And for some forty plus years, the first black immigrants held property, sued in court, and accumulated pounds and plantations as did whites. But as we all know too well, this all changed dramatically in the seventeenth century, when many of our founding fathers, spurred-on by greed and the unprotected status of Africans, enacted laws which reduced most would-be African-Americans to lives of slavery.

What does this have to do with anything, you ask? Well, centuries later, many of today's African-Americans are wondering if history is attempting to repeat itself.

There appears to be a growing amount of greed, jealousy, and resentment over the slowly evolving, seemingly prospering status of today's middle-class African-Americans. And once again, these things seem to be spurring many people to do as America and our founding fathers did before, in what is now called our shameful past.

This is significant, as today, it is almost again proving to be fashionable to express or exemplify views which are considered "conservative," a word often used as a code name for, not exactly helping racial minorities, and I put that as nicely as I could. So, as this phenomenon seems to be sweeping our nation, a real hard look must be given before action is taken. You might just be surprised at what is actually discovered.

White, Male & Discriminated Against

Today, as white males increasingly are claiming to be victimized by affirmative action and set aside programs, talk of the "Angry White Male" has grown to a fever pitch. These men say that affirmative action and set asides take what should be theirs, and simply gives it to unqualified blacks.

These men say that they are losing pay raises, promotions, educational opportunities, and the American Dream.

But despite such political rhetoric, which often pits blacks and whites against one another, neither group is really a primary recipient of governmental affirmative action. And all of this when historically, special breaks such as affirmative action and race-based preferences have been as American as apple pie, drawing criticism only when used to assist blacks, or other minorities. We know that the largest federal "breaks" have traditionally, and continue to go to wealthy individuals, large corporations, farmers, ranchers, and miners--virtually all *white males*. So why the fuss by white males?

We know that blacks were intentionally held back in our country, while everyone else advanced forward. In fact, for a long period of time, it was even against the law for blacks to be educated. And when blacks were educated, various municipal laws still literally prohibited blacks from practicing in certain occupations, as it was made a crime in many areas. Today, these first generation professionals are expected to compete equally against those who have traditions of excelling for many generations, with no oppressive hold-backs.

So, as blacks were hampered by deliberate oppression, coupled with white fears, racism, and prejudice, all which still runs through today, what would you propose be done to honor the Constitution's promise of life, liberty, and the pursuit of happiness for those who we know are discriminated against? What measures would you put into place? Surely you would wish to create social justice, and make the world a better place to live in, right? This is why affirmative action has been in existence.

Now, the author understands that not all white males inherited land, money and other forms of financial security left to them by ancestors who virtually "tied up the competition," and unfairly made out like bandits. However, no matter how one looks at the situation, though other Americans were discriminated against (Jews, Italians, Irish, Japanese, Chinese...), no other ethnic groups have ever been as brutally oppressed, or "cheated against" as blacks. This has given most whites large, staunch head starts over blacks. This is so, as in essence, whites were given large leads, as black's arms and legs were tied. After whites developed huge leads, virtually guaranteeing that whites would "win the race," then blacks had their arms and legs untied, and were told, "Okay, now the race is fair, start."

With affirmative action, as the average white male was given a 75-100 yard head start in a 400 yard race, affirmative action simply cut the head start down by 10 yards. And white women, many of whom already had access to capital from well-to-do relatives, etcetera, and who previously had as much as a 25-50 yard head start, were given an extra 10 yards.

So, as preferential treatment for white males has long been wide- spread, America's wealth has also been multiplied with the exploitation of blacks, and taking the property rights of Indian lands. In the late 1800's, many whites became quite wealthy, *uncompetitively*, due to the Homestead Act, which literally gave free homesteads of more than one-million acres of soil and oil-rich land, to white males who were war veterans. But, although blacks had fought in every war since the American Revolution, they did not qualify. And the Indian people, though it was rightfully their land in the first place, also did not qualify to settle the land in which generations of their people had grown-up on.

People are all aware of the white male-dominated institutions such as the media, finance, advertising, law, academia, and Hollywood. All of these institutions, and these are just a representative few, use informal hiring and/or promotion preferences. Leaders within these institutions often hire and promote people who look like them, live in their neighborhoods, and attend their clubs and organizations. And what's wrong with this picture? Blacks and women are usually not admittedly a part of these groups. So therefore, the old buddy system ends up ensuring a quota of about the present 90%-95% white males at the top--now that's affirmative action!

And with regard to contracts, on a frequent basis, the author has encountered countless minority-owned companies with as good and/or better products as the "big guys." Many of these companies often have had solid experience, were less expensive in price, were very professional, intelligent, did good work, etc., and even made great presentations. But never, and I mean never, has the author seen any of these companies, with the exception of janitorial services companies, and those firms owned by white women, receive any contracts, especially professional services contracts, worth more than just a few thousand dollars. The exception of course, was if a bloody, knockdown, drag-out battle was first fought. And even then, many of these firms were still not awarded contracts. Had these been white firms, there is no doubt that like today, law suits would have flown all over the place, unlike the case with these minority firms.

Just look at it this way. If you take an ad agency for instance, let's say that firm A is pursuing a large bank as a client. This firm is small, owned by a "real minority," produces excellent, high-quality work, with quick turnarounds, does so at a competitive price, and is a wonderful firm across the board. However, firm B is the present ad agency for this bank, is large, white-owned, has been in existence for 25 years, and utilizes the bank as its bank, running nearly $20 million per year through it, but the advertising is stale. Now, even with stale advertising, who do you think will likely get or keep the account? That's right, the stale advertiser, firm B, even though firm A is "qualified," a superior advertiser, and produces better work. This type of situation is prevalent everyday throughout our society.

So, if people wonder, these types of reasons are why affirmative action has been deemed necessary. Many would argue that if whites had to endure what blacks must endure, undoubtedly, we would currently have much stronger programs in existence than what affirmative action measures currently provide.

The author knows that a *few* success stories do exist, but they are certainly the exception, and definitely not the rule. Remember the statistics, 56% of all black-owned businesses receive less than $10,000 per year, less than half of what non-black, women-owned businesses take in.

So, for the record, it should be stated that yes, blacks will be hurt by abolishing affirmative action, but you've seen the statistics, who has benefitted the most? So let us not act too hastily. The fact is that though blacks have taken much of the heat for affirmative action, its abolition will hurt the many more white women which it has helped. Abolishing this program will also hurt many white men, and white-owned companies as well. What? That's right, you read correctly.

One reason is because blacks spend such a large portion of their disposable incomes with white-owned companies (approximately 98%). Another reason is that many white males benefit either through black's purchases, or through their wive's attainments of contracts due to affirmative action programs. And as the big guys usually gobble-up everything else, what makes white male small business owners think that they would benefit even if affirmative action was eradicated? At best, these men would only have a small, crab-like victory, meaning, "If I can't get the business, then you shouldn't either." So, the main problem facing all working people today, including white males, is not affirmative action, its corporate greed--fueled largely because of greedy, rich investors.

In fact, before I could even complete this book, AT&T had already announced that it would eliminate 40,000 jobs over the next three years. Its stock market price jumped 2 7/8 points, or increased by $4 billion in value for investors, in one day. But AT&T is just one of many such organizations, as 1995's mergers and acquisitions totaled nearly $600 billion. So just why are companies cutting back? Good question.

Corporate profits are at record highs, worker's productivity continues to climb, and the stock market continues to earn record highs, yet employers continue to cut wages and benefits of employees, and worse, shift millions of decent paying jobs outside of the United States, where they make most of their money--The New World Order?

Are these companies in danger of going out-of-business? No, not hardly. They are just firing Americans to simply make more money.

As corporations shift many remaining full-time jobs to part-time or temporary positions, without benefits, and with others shipping jobs out of the U.S., to where workers are paid only a few dollars per day, corporate profits and stock market highs mean little to the overall economy for most everyday Americans.

This area is where "Angry White Males" should place their misguided anger. These men should not be cowardly, and place their anger on small, low-impact areas like affirmative action.

Important Issues

One of the only reasons why the U.S. has not yet slipped into a recession already, is because the Federal Reserve has recognized our economic woes, and has lowered interest rates to keep the economy limping along, and blacks in particular, have kept buying. So, while people are buying new homes because of lower interest rates, the real question in America today is, how long will these people have decent paying jobs to pay for these new homes?

If it were not for the Fed's actions, we would all be feeling much more of a pinch right now, so it's good there was monetary policy intervention, for the Olympics was coming to a major U.S. city. And despite many Americans not being able to afford to go to the Olympics, at least our city didn't appear to be a ravished, poor communist nation--at least not yet. After all, how long can low interest rates sustain us when everything about the middle-class is being eroded? And don't forget, today's war-torn Bosnia (the former Yugoslavia) hosted the Olympics not long ago too.

The moral to this story? Many people's priorities are in the wrong places. Blacks and affirmative action are not our problem. And besides, if black consumers are hurt, then sooner or later, the effects will be felt by whites too, sooner rather than later.

So let's put it all in perspective. It should be noted that currently, ways exist in which discrimination is entirely possible, which can never legally be proven. It is virtually the same as what Cain did to Able in the Bible, and no one saw but God. So while not all, *some* whites in fact are attempting to economically neutralize or "kill" their brothers, though the so-called "Christian Coalition," "Religious Right" or whatever they call themselves, appears not to be addressing this point at all. And let us not also forget that many hate and Neo-Nazi groups are also called Christian White Supremacists. Should this tell us anything? The Bible tells us that there will be those who wrap themselves in "religious cloaks," but will essentially be of the Devil's synagogue. So, I state this not to negatively address anyone in particular, but this is to say that we all need to keep our eyes and ears open.

What does that mean? It means that people cannot be gullible enough to assume that simply because someone says he's religious, we should follow him. That would make us easy victims, and we are all familiar with the Beast noted in the Bible. And as some religious scholars believe that the Beast is alive and among us today, such credulous practices should be seen as dangerous, for they could easily contribute to the great demise of the United States.

Anyway, relating back to the earlier phrase of some whites wishing to economically neutralize or "kill" their brothers. As some within the "Christian Right" would concur, the Bible also reads, "If someone says, 'I love God,' and hates his brother, he is a liar; for he who does not love his brother whom he has seen, how can he love God whom he has not seen?" (1 John 4:20). This scripture should speak volumes to us all, in and of itself.

Let us not forget that Jesus was a Jew, yet many who call themselves *Christ*ians, hate Jews. In fact, if Jesus was unknowingly again among us today, but perhaps this time came as a black man, it is this author's belief that many so-called Christians, both black and white, would once again crucify Jesus, while other church-going, so-called Christians would again, simply watch him be crucified, and do nothing. I wonder how many people are really going to Heaven?

But anyway, as many black persons believe that in an environment which is often racist in thought and behavior, greedy, hostile, and the like, blacks would seem to have very little chance at gaining opportunities without at least some type of affirmative action. Recent times seem to be proving this true.

Though this author is not confident that affirmative action will live beyond the next few years, the author does not necessarily agree that this should be the case. So as such, various important factors in this chapter should at least be explained, and reviewed by you.

It's About Time For The Facts

Before we draw any further brash conclusions about affirmative action, set-asides, who's the most qualified, etc., stimulated by little more than extremist, unfounded rhetoric, let's take a close analysis of the facts for ourselves.

Many people argue that blacks were qualified to play in the major leagues before Jackie Robinson. Many were even qualified to be on Capitol Hill, as slaves freed since 1863, went to college, were progressive, and received Ph.D's. In 1895, there were even 22 black congressmen, and a black middle-class. But much like today, the courts began to act swiftly, and as an oppressive mood swept the country, by 1901, there wasn't one single black on Capitol Hill. This would last for the next 29 years!

Blacks were qualified to share rest rooms and ride buses with whites before the 1960's. Blacks were even qualified to sell hamburgers for McDonalds, chicken for KFC and soft drinks for Coca-Cola, before these companies finally and reluctantly began to hire a *few* of these people in management positions in the 1970's. The list goes on, but the point is that blacks and women have been qualified to do a lot of things for a long-time, but were simply not given the opportunity to bat, or compete on the same level playing field. In fact, the playing field on which most blacks have been playing is set on a virtually ninety degree angle. So, as the doors of opportunity were not opened then, despite being qualified, what makes us think that the future will be any brighter? After all, history does repeat itself.

So let's face it, in all honesty, being qualified is not the real issue, though that has been a clever argument from many who wish for affirmative action's abolition. But the bottom line is that though many African-Americans wish they did not need some sort of affirmative action, many know that without it, they will once again be locked-out of America's creed of "Life, liberty, and the pursuit of happiness," due to little more than lack of fairness, injustice, and race-related suppression. So what other alternatives are there?

Anti-affirmative action arguments do *sound* good. But the real issue is that many white males are no longer guaranteed a better life, despite having college degrees. For in remembering the alleged good ole' days, this was largely the case with the generation before. In fact, surprisingly enough, while compiling research, the author learned that even today, many white corporate executives of large corporate bodies, do not have college degrees, despite those qualifications being a pre-requisite for blacks at the same companies, in the same positions. So as such, with continuing corporate cut-backs, many white males are scared out-of-their-minds of what fate awaits them, even if affirmative action is done away with.

With jobs being slashed by the tens of thousands, decimating the middle-class of both blacks and whites, and despite corporate record earnings, it appears that the future will ultimately turn into a desperate struggle between rich and poor, rather than just black and white. It's ironic, because today's environment seems to be turning those once futuristic Sci-Fi movies into today's realities--cellular phones, cars with on-board navigation systems, watches which you talk into... They're all images from science fiction movies. And if this trend continues to where science fiction becomes reality, and there is no sign of change on the horizon, then we are all not far from times when rich greedy guys control everything, complete with their own private armies, high-tech weapons, etcetera--fighting against poorly armed rebels, both black and white, just like in the movies. And as Congress seems to be heading us in that direction, by giving giants more latitude to "slay David", then the possibility of something like this seems more and more real everyday, especially today. However, this brings me to another very important topic.

Extraordinary Crisis

Since 1969, America's wealthiest 20% of the population has gotten steadily and significantly wealthier, increasing its wealth more than 39% since 1969. This means that a mere 1% of our population now controls more than 46% of our nation's wealth! Twelve percent of our nation controls nearly 80%, and only 20% of our population now owns and controls more than 86% of our nation's wealth!

As new Republican-backed congressional plans are introduced, wealth for this elitist group is expected to grow even more so in the future. So, if this should happen, and I currently see no reasons why it will not, then wealth disparity in the U.S. between rich and poor, will continue to become greater than it has ever been, as is already the case.

With stagnating wages since 1987, and decreasing real wages, this trend will eventually give people little choice but to fight fiercely and openly against the rich elite and irresponsible, greedy big businesses, or starve, literally.

For the first time in several decades, it appears that the backbone of America, the middle-class, will suffer dramatically.

The Mortgage Bankers Association in Washington, D.C., recently released a report stating that past due mortgages were behind more in 1995 than at any other time in the last four years. And with consumers leveraged with credit card debt, that brings the number of debt-holding Americans and the amount of debt being held by Americans to an all time high. The number of personal bankruptcies in America has also skyrocketed.

So we are in an era where the corporate "cut-throat" trend is on the rise, and this will mean that millions of middle-class, employed, well-educated, high-wage earners and professionals, will soon become unemployed, underemployed, and placed in the position that most blacks have been placed in for so long. And sadly enough, most of these people will have few options to fall back on.

Almost in the blink of an eye, small businesses will collapse, houses and cars will be lost, most kids won't have jobs after graduating from college, if they're able to go to college, and at the same time, the stock market will likely continue to soar, while thousands of people will have more money than they could ever spend in several life times.

What I am stating is the harsh reality which awaits us, even if affirmative action is removed from the system. But one thing's for certain, if affirmative action is abolished, surely *everyone* will lose. The only exceptions would be the richest 20% or so of our nation. In fact, not only will the rich not lose, but this elite group will gain. How? I'm glad you asked.

Strategic Communications Activities

As extraordinary wealth and sainthood have not exactly gone hand-in-hand traditionally, then what is happening today should be of no surprise to anyone. You see, the power, and ultimately perhaps the wealth of our richest 20%, is greatly threatened right now. This is so as women are demanding more power, fairness and independence these days, and so are blacks, hispanics and other groups. All are demanding fairness, and in essence, they are seeking to share in the balance of power.

This is a problem though, because the only way to maintain absolute power is through political venues. And as the majority appears to be unhappy with the status-quo right now, the only way for rich persons to maintain their control is to create social instability, wearing people down, and taking their attention away from issues which might otherwise unify traditionally non-unified groups.

So drawing from my expertise as an advertising, marketing and public relations professional, please allow me to share with you a bit about marketing and public relations.

In my profession, when something does not look good, the first thing we do is to divert attention away from that particular issue. And in order to do this on a large scale, a plan must be devised--perhaps a written plan, but nonetheless, a plan, whether produced by an individual or group. This is the case today. I know this, as I have employed similar tricks myself to get clients out of frying pans. None of my tricks have been this diabolical, but roughly speaking, they have been from the same bag.

The outcome? Time and time again, such tactics worked beautifully. This is why *some* PR professionals recognize this strategy from a mile away. Why it's one of our own "tricks." This strategic "plan" undoubtedly is to utilize mass communications, the world's most influential tool, to rid many of the social and political elite of the threat made today by women and minorities. Sound crazy? Not so fast before you decide.

You see, in case you are unfamiliar with advertising and marketing planning, an analysis of a situation must first take place. This analysis usually identifies the strongest and weakest points of attack, then they are acted upon. So as business is politics, wouldn't such a close relationship between wealthy persons and politicians seem to suggest that those with money, rely upon politicians to help them keep it, as well as their considerable influence?

A sitting U.S. House of Representatives member must raise approximately $5,000 per week, for every week he or she is in office, just so he or she can be re-elected. So with this much money needed, doesn't this seem to suggest that individuals and entities with lots of money can buy influence, and even votes from *our* so-called politicians? And after thinking about it, this would make one wonder, are politicians really ours, or do we just think they are?

The bottom line is that in order to maintain the status-quo, and keep alive some families' traditions of continuing to virtually run the country, and the government, a heated topical debate such as the affirmative action debate, had to be created, exploited, and used as smoke and mirrors.

As an individual who has pulled the rabbit out of the hat a few times while using smoke and mirrors myself, I think that makes me at least just a little bit qualified to share this insight with you.

Today's affirmative action debate is a clever communications technique designed to make people believe certain things, while other things that are not revealed, are really going on. We've all had suspicions about such things, but simply couldn't prove them. But since the average person cannot randomly cut someone open to prove that their brain controls their thoughts, reasonable logic, some degree of common sense, and trust of people who have practiced in such an area makes us believe that this is so.

And though we cannot see him, touch him, smell him or physically hear him, does this make most of us eager to denounce that there is a God in heaven? No. So, what's wrong with knowing something, but not being able to physically "prove" it? After all, the biggest trick that Satin ever played on the world was in convincing the world that he does not exist.

So why would some people outside of politicians and our rich elite grossly deny that this is the case in this instance? Because for starters, many people are scared, and simply wish not to believe that something this fiendish could be true, even if it is. Many mostly middle-class individuals will simply hide behind the shield of "Well, it can't be proven," and the like. However, that is an intellectually weak argument, for we all know that even if a person is a notorious mobster, if he eliminates witnesses, then a case cannot be physically *proven*. That does not necessarily mean that the mobster never committed the crime, however.

So the bottom line? The current affirmative action debate is a deliberate, designed diversion which has been derived politically, and intentionally implemented to take timely advantage of the emotions of today's working-class white males, many of whom we call today's Angry White Males.

These men are important to this equation. They are considered foot soldiers, or ground troops, a necessary part of any such expedition. The exploitation of these men, and their support, at least for right now, is imperative to the continuance of the status-quo. This is what keeps most people in the middle-class or less, and others poor and powerless, except of course, those who already have extreme wealth and power, and who happen to like it.

More On Strategic Communications Activities

In advertising, we appeal to people's emotions. If we do that, then we've got a sale--fear, anger, whatever type of emotion, it doesn't matter--the technique is still the same. So as many white males right now feel vulnerable, this is precisely how *some* of our congressmen and elite who are "at the top," wish to see these men feel. No wonder why thousands of 19 year employees are being let go and tossed-out from companies at the drop of a hat, despite corporate profits reigning high. After all, the same wealthy stockholders usually own large chunks of several different companies.

The ripple effects of such activities can be devastating, and as such, wallagh, you have a group of angry white males, ready to find direction so they can go attack someone.

Many do not know any better. After all, after being caught-up in such an emotional whirl wind, it is only natural that people react the way that many white males have, especially when they believe that their problems exist because of affirmative action, like they are told.

Often times, these are the things that these men are often told right before they are given the boot, or are turned down for employment. After all, it is sometimes just plain easier, socially speaking, to tell a person that they didn't get a job because of hiring quotas, than it is to tell them they really weren't qualified. It likely furthers many persons' social agendas of maintaining dominant positioning in the marketplace, while also alleviating the stress of telling people that they weren't selected--killing two birds with one stone.

The author has developed several strategic plans over time, and I can tell you all of the makings of a good plan when I see one. This is one such plan. I'd like for people to remember just one thing, if you don't already know. In politics, *nothing* happens by sheer accident or coincidence. Politics is the epitome of Sun Tsu, the art of warfare, meaning that every battle in politics is won before it is ever fought. And being smart in politics means simply knowing when to pull a trigger. Think about it. Anyone significant who has ever nearly become successful in helping to create fairness, social and racial equality in America, has always been shot--Abraham Lincoln, Martin Luther King, Jr., Malcolm X, and John F. Kennedy, just to name a few. Should this not tell us something?

I do not suggest that all white people are bad people. In fact, some have been very helpful in attempting to ensure justice and fairness for blacks. So, with this being the case, then ask yourself, who would be the beneficiaries of ending affirmative action? Blue collar, beer drinking white guys? No, if these guys don't have the technological skills to keep pace with most industries, they will naturally be left behind. Will middle-class white guys benefit? No, these guys likely will be hurt as a result--loose jobs due to black's spending stops with companies, close small businesses due to the ripple effects, and still lose corporate jobs with a spending slowdown by blacks. So, who would benefit from the abolition of affirmative action?

Answer that question, and you will have revealed the rascals--many of our rich elite, and selfish or ambitious congressional politicians, essentially "hired" by some of our rich elite to help them protect *their* interests. And we can bet that interests of the rich cannot be protected if people traditionally from outside of the "ole' boy network" are allowed to gain power. In case you don't understand, you'll see what I mean a little later in this text.

Talk About Preferences

The reality of today, even with affirmative action on the books, is that many black business owners continue to struggle. Black students face continued hurdles when seeking educations, black workers, especially black males, feel the crunch of experiencing an unemployment rate twice that of whites, and on top of that, these men often hold dead-end, labor-intensive, low-paying jobs, even with higher levels of education than their white counterparts. So, these types of situations hardly support many of the wide-spread claims that we hear spouted about today.

While affirmative action has opened doors for some African-Americans, it is their ability that gets them inside. After all, no one whom the author has come into contact with has had any big breaks because they were black. And these are only a few of millions of African-Americans just like them. Despite an accelerated rate of blacks graduating from colleges and universities with degrees, most end up settling for something much, much less than what they hoped for when they graduate.

In 1990, although more than 45 percent of blacks age 16+ had at least some college education, less than 25 percent were employed in professional fields, according to the U.S. Department of Labor. So, this too runs counter to the common gripe which has been heard in Corporate America for years: "There just aren't enough qualified blacks to hire and promote. We would if we could find them."

According to the U.S. Department of Education, there was more than a 35 percent increase in blacks ages 20 to 44, with college degrees. The federal bi-partisan Glass Ceiling Commission also reported that it is evident that there is a pool of African-American college graduates, which has increased in the past decade. It has also been found by the federal bi-partisan labor commission, that after three years of study, a glass ceiling does still exist not only for women in our country, but also for blacks as well.

So while it should be noted that some gains have been made by women, both black, white, and others, on the other hand, it is doubtful that as many opportunities have been made available to black males. Why do you think this is so?

As we just discussed that the future looks bleak for almost everyone, whether affirmative action is eradicated or not, then is such a battle even worth fighting? Where is the real battle which should be fought? Well, let's look at it this way. Since much debate has recently surfaced regarding wealthy persons having a ceiling put upon the amount they can spend to defend themselves in capital murder cases, shouldn't we take it a step further? Shouldn't we help-out middle America by perhaps assigning a 50% tax to incomes of every *individual* with say $100 million or more?

This would certainly make your tax burden, your neighbor's, mine, and so on, greatly less burdensome. After all, more middle- Americans would benefit by being able to form their own businesses, and continue to employ others, where 90% of all American workers are currently employed--the true backbone of American society--not major trickle-down economics, which the past and present shows us just does not work.

The middle-class has been paying the bulk of the taxes for all of this time, so why not finally give this group a break and have those who can afford it, pay more. But oh, I forgot. That would mean that extremely wealthy individuals could then buy only one helicopter instead of two, and could only afford a moderate billionaire's yacht, instead of the biggest in the world. Excuse me, what was I thinking?

So the bottom line is, when economists are truthful with themselves, by enacting such a measure, outside of hurting multi-millionaire and billionaire egos, no one would really get hurt, and the middle-class, our most important body, would surely gain. The only snag is that our elite would somehow try to get vindictive, and do something to thwart such a thing.

The rich would still remain rich, and "ordinary citizens" would finally begin to see some economic justice. I also bet that if more of our elite's money was being spent by the government, there would come to be less government waste, and our politicians wouldn't continue taking so many expensive trips either.

Besides, our elite wouldn't exactly starve to death. And to satisfy their capitalistic urges for making more money, well, they'd receive half of what they make over $100 million, not bad. And besides, this would benefit the average, "common person," transcending ultimately to society at large. Do I think that the government spends too much on waste? Yes, I do. But, if more of the rich's money was being spent, you would probably see government waste cut tremendously, because these people wouldn't stand for large sums of *their* money being wasted.

So, what I am suggesting is that if the rich were more active as watchdogs of tax dollars, rather than turning the other way, because senators keep *their* tax bills low, this would benefit America. And last but not least, Americans pay less in taxes than any of the other westernized countries which rival the U.S. anyway. Hence, a 50% tax on those with $100 million would be no more than what other western nations already pay.

Although the author recognizes that economic growth must be an integral factor of our nation's overall prosperity, one thing is for certain, our nation will never prosper as long as the middle- class continues to be burdened with most of the taxes, and less of the rewards. Again, we now know from history that trickle-down economics just does not work. So, growth strategies, coupled with *liveable wages*, and middle-class tax relief is the only direction in which to travel. And besides, such a philosophy coincides with the Biblical saying, "all things in moderation," and that includes capitalism.

If some of our wealthiest citizens were such patriots, and were *really* interested in creating jobs and saving American families like they tout, then many would do so without necessarily having to receive a millionaire's capital gains cut in the process. Wouldn't you agree?

And as wealthy franchise owners and others who earn nearly a million dollars per year or more in profits, but argue that they can't afford to pay their workers, in which 63% of them are single mothers with children, more than $4.25 per hour, or less than $9,000 per year, before taxes, without cutting jobs, then the author suggests that those jobs just be cut. The reason is because if people can't earn an honorable, decent living by working hard everyday, then these capitalists are doing little to contribute to the well-being of our society, at all. Perhaps the government should subsidize this for low-income small businesses, to off-set inflation. Even if the deficit took a few months or a year longer to eliminate by going this route, it would be well worth it.

But regardless, if a regular, 40 hour per week plus job cannot pay an individual at least $10,000-$12,000 per year, then this author believes that such a job is not worth creating. This comes from a man who has worked for such meager wages, unlike most opposing congressmen. My reasoning for this statement? Even with such a job, if the wage is not liveable enough to actually pay taxes, and provide basic necessities, with us having to spend substantially more money, between $25,000 per year and $60,000 per year, to house each prisoner who commits often desperate crimes in pursuit of earning enough to provide a minimum, decent standard of living for their families, in the richest nation on earth, then that job has done nothing to aid our society.

Besides, the bottom line is that with a larger, more prosperous middle-class, everyone wins. But the richest 20% who ultimately profit from the status-quo, including racial tensions, say no thanks, because many would frankly prefer to see everyone kill themselves before they would dare to be left with only a measly hundred million dollars, or whatever. Such capitalistic resistance in essence, parallels us with the dreadful days of sharecropping.

We have issues such as this to consider, so why are people fighting over low-impact issues such as affirmative action? As a member of today's Generation X, tomorrow's societal backbone, this concerns me greatly.

IMPORTANT CONSIDERATIONS INVOLVING AFFIRMATIVE ACTION & SET ASIDES

Who's More Qualified Anyway?

Often times, many white males unknowingly, but often disdainfully respond that a higher score on a standardized test automatically makes them more qualified than African-Americans or women. What do you think? Do you agree? Well, before you answer, first, consider the following and figure it into your intellectual equation.

One basic difference between blacks and whites is as we discussed before, perception--some things appearing different than what they might seem to really be.

In advertising, we know that of all the people in the U.S., approximately 45% are left brain thinkers, 45% are right brain thinkers, and 10% are both. Now, this is important, as on the average, it appears that a majority of white males in particular, have well-trained "left brains." Persons who are left brain thinkers, often are persons who are very analytical and strategic in nature. These persons are often good in subjects like mathematics and science, love to read, see options in black and white, and are often shrewd negotiators and the like.

On the other hand, on the average, it appears that a majority of African-Americans often appear to be right brain thinkers. And as you may know, persons who are right brain thinkers, usually are very creative in nature. These people usually do not see options only in black and white. They often can imagine the future before it even happens, pushing creativity to its outer limits. So what does all of this have to do with anything? Allow me to explain.

Have you ever noticed that people who are extremely good in mathematics usually are not fond of subjects like English for instance? Or noticed that persons who excel at subjects like English, usually dislike advanced math? It's true, and it's usually because of their brain dominance-- the side of the brain which appears to have been "trained" the most.

While I am not a psychologist, a great part of my job as a marketing professional is observing and evaluating psychological behavior. As such, from my numerous observations, it appears true that virtually all persons are capable of excelling at most things--if they begin training early enough at least. It all boils down to the old cliche', "practice makes perfect."

It also appears that many African-Americans, as children, usually grow-up performing activities which "train" the right side, or creative side of their brains. Thus, they can often do unimaginable things on the basketball court, have great hand and eye coordination, develop things which we now know as rock-n-roll, rap and hip-hop, and invent things as often as the wind blows, often times even with little or no formal education or training.

Many white males, on the other hand, as youngsters, usually perform activities which "train" the left side or analytical side of their brains. Thus, these children can often formulate strategic principles which might excel in business, and focus very well on things such as company expansions or cost reductions when they become adults. These things all appear to come natural for both right brain and left brain thinking groups.

And take women for instance. Ever noticed how well women seem to be able to read people? If you haven't noticed, then maybe you should, because it's true. Women often tend to be very detail oriented, compared with men, who often times tend to only be concerned with the big picture. For men at least, whether black or white, the theory is that this is caused because of culturalization. With women, however, while the environment would appear obvious, numerous studies have been done, which seem to suggest that levels of testosterone may be the case here.

Ponder this for a moment. Most analytical persons can usually help to perfect something, and often times guide it along through its development. However, these individuals will usually have little to perfect, if someone does not first create or develop an idea or concept for them.

Thus, wouldn't it appear that such an analytical person could greatly benefit from having a creative person who is strong in areas where he is weak, on his team? It would appear that these people could be much more effective by teaming up with one another under these circumstances. Sounds like a potential dynamic-duo. And this should be considered as something to add to the affirmative action debate.

While affirmative action appears to have some sort of legal consequence associated with it, the issue of blacks and whites complementing one another doesn't, so perhaps this should prominently be addressed with the changing demographics which persists in the United States.

Although many white males believe that we are "over doing diversity," that is likely only because they do not understand what the reality as opposed to the theory of diversity actually means. Having diversity does not mean addressing legal concerns or moral issues, it is business, economics, and all of the above. The sooner we all understand this fact, the better-off we will all be. As Dr. Martin Luther King, Jr. once stated, "If we do not all learn to live together as human beings, we will all surely die like fools."

In a nutshell is this, Japan has once again taken advantage of an American first, which we have discarded, and they've perfected it. What they have done is to maximize and utilize their best creative persons, and couple them with analytical minds to create an economic powerhouse with their products, now rivaling the rest of the western world. Remember when people used to laugh at the made in Japan tags on products? Do you reckon that those same people are laughing now? Such success would too be America, if only we were not so arrogant about issues of race, sex, and making more money at all costs.

So why after all of this time, has America not realized its rich, hidden treasures, and taken advantage of them? After all, as most things in our universe usually have a cause and effect relationship, then wouldn't it seem possible that mother nature intentionally designed us to be interdependent upon one another?

And accepting the premise that this is so, then this would also mean that the potential collapse or demise of one group, as best-selling author Dr. Dennis Waitley points out in his book, *Empires of The Mind*, would mean the ultimate eradication of the other.

So yes, America *is* truly uniquely blessed like no other country in the world, to have such a rich diversity of people, coming from various cultures, each with something different and significant to contribute--a place where different cultures often means different outlooks, and different outlooks often leads to new and improved innovations. Whether acknowledged or not, this diversity has surged the United States to its upward advancement throughout time.

Without blacks, perhaps we would have no light bulbs, for the filaments were created by a black man, perhaps our nation's capital, Washington, D.C., would not be as attractive, were it not for its designer, a black man. We would not have had blood plasma available to allied troops during World War II, or even the telephone, were it not for the innovation of black men. The list goes on, but hopefully, you get the point.

Some persons have been immensely creative, many of them African-Americans, whether noted or not. And other people have been excellent money managers, had excellent strategic directional skills, negotiations and the like. It is very difficult for any one person to possess all of these traits--

why it would be the perfect person, and we all know that there is no such being.

Although some might disagree, even in modern academia, very little reward is usually handed-out for creativity. Rewards are rather usually reserved for analytical abilities instead.

You see, with the increased presence of women on college campuses over the years, such defects have been realized, as more institutions have begun to become more liberal arts academies than anything else. But the recognition of creativity is still far less than what it should be in our country, and in this author's opinion, this is also seriously contributing to our nation's decline.

Thus, I have stated all of that to state that in some instances, white males may in fact perform better on standardized tests than blacks and women. After all, as you likely know, many standardized tests are often from a white male slanted view point, and virtually require a background rich with white culturalization. The only exception is the math section, which is the only area which is universal. As such, this obviously would place virtually any African-American at a disadvantage coming from his or her own culture. And this system basically guarantees that whoever has the greatest white culturalization, wins the game, so who do we predict that the winners would be?

Needless to say, such should not serve as a sole benchmark, or anything of the sort, for if the same people who did well on these tests were tested for their creative abilities, many would fail miserably. So to answer the question, should a standardized test determine a "winner?" Absolutely not. No one factor by itself should determine something so crucial. Just as with most data analysis, the data may infer one thing, but a skilled person may interpret that the data means something else. Such is also the case with standardized tests.

Let me put it to you another way. This is the same scenario as an average white guy attempting to beat Michael Jordan in a game of basketball. It simply can't be done, and we should not expect African-Americans, who are playing the role of the "white guy" in this example, to "beat Michael Jordan" in a game where the deck is so stacked up against them.

So one thing is for certain, if we continue to use standardized test criteria as a sole judge to determine a "winner," America will surely become the loser.

The History Of Affirmative Action

So that readers may have a better understanding, please allow me to share more about the background of affirmative action with you.

During the early 1970's, African-Americans seemed to finally begin to be making at least some rebounds for virtually the first time since the Reconstruction Era. And the reason was due in great part to what is today referred to as affirmative action.

The background of affirmative action, set asides and race-based scholarship programs, are that they came into existence, due to widespread discrimination, which was aimed largely at blacks. Thus, it was perceived that unless some type of progressive assistance was put into place, the oppressive forces which had kept most blacks in American society's doldrums for so many years, would continue to oppress and stifle the advancement of blacks in America. This type of oppression stood against everything being an American stood for, and it was viewed that such oppression was too destructive for our nation as a whole, as it damned us all, and had to be challenged head-on.

Many intellectuals, including President Kennedy, believed that as history being the judge, American white males being a majority, would likely not be willing to voluntarily and fairly open the playing field to those who did not look like white males. This stood as a type of protectionism, which America has always fought hard against, and could not be allowed to persist in our nation's own back yard.

If things remained the same, power would then virtually only be bestowed because of two factors, race, and sex, rendering all others basically powerless. These intellectuals believed that such would be like a cancer of the most dangerous and malignant kind, and that we should not render power to a group and virtual poverty and exclusion to another, based upon little more reasoning than a person's race and sex. They were right. Such a tactic has been used for centuries, to keep those 20% of Americans who were in power yesterday, in power today, and such thought was viewed as evil, yet genius, for it has worked so dreadfully well.

These men knew that even for the sake of argument, if whites did voluntarily allow blacks to share in the American spirited process, all of the decks would still remain stacked against blacks, in favor of whites, leaving many blacks with almost insurmountable odds in which to battle, making fair American competition virtually impossible.

So the principle of affirmative action was put into existence by President Kennedy in 1961, requiring firms holding federal contracts to increase the employment of minorities. The number and scope of such programs increased following the passage of the 1964 Civil Rights Act and Equal Employment Opportunity Act of 1972. Nonetheless, it is important to note that affirmative action is and never was a law. It was and is but a principle, which provided us with goals--goals in which since their implementation during the late 1960's, have never before come close to being reached in the history of U.S. federal procurement contracts, until 1994. For the first time in U.S. history, under the Clinton Administration, more federal contracts were awarded to women, blacks, hispanics, and other minorities, collectively, than at any other time in U.S. history. Yet, this was still below 10%.

However, during the 1970's, opposition grew as the programs spread, and there were numerous court challenges by opponents. The U.S. Supreme Court gave approval to affirmative action in one significant ruling, the case of Regents of the University of California v. Bakke (1978). The Court held that race could be a factor in selecting applicants for admission to universities, but indicated that rigid quotas were unacceptable.

This ruling was acceptable, as affirmative action did no more than provide goals. But because so many companies had been defiant in the past, and waited so late in the game to hire minorities in the first place, a desperate scramble then ensued to hire blacks, which people now refer to as filling quotas.

Over time, whites seemed to become ashamed of the wretched treatment blacks had received, and the hearts of many began to weigh heavy through the 1960's. Many whites empathized with the unfair struggles most blacks endured, and the hatred many whites had seen first-hand shown against blacks. With regard to such hatred, the reasons for it were so questionable, that even most whites could not understand why it persisted. And in fact, to this very day, many people still cannot reasonably answer the question of why black persons are hated by many whites, even those blacks whom these people have never met or spoken with.

Thus, with the change in attitudes of a nation, came a change in the nation itself, for the better--for a little while.

Approximately twenty-five years later, the strength which is obtained from meeting such heavy resistance, somehow, managed to birth many successful, present day African-Americans. But because of so many unfavorable factors, many of today's successful African-Americans likely would not have been given the chances and opportunities to advance, and further their careers, had it not ultimately been for affirmative action. This is not to state that these people did not work hard to get where they are, however. For in fact, quite the opposite is true. Many were largely or wholly self-educated, and most blacks had to always be twice as good as their white counterparts, just in order to at least get the *chance* to get the promotion or job. However, as America evolved, many blacks evolved too.

In the area of government contracts, many have been grandfathered or simply inherited by large companies, not subject to any qualifications tests of being the best qualified, most cost competitive, etcetera. And historically speaking, it is difficult to see why America has never been outraged in these instances.

Another situation which has drawn steam from blacks, is when sons, daughters, nephews, nieces and cousins of influential, wealthy white men get accepted to good colleges, and get hired or promoted over everyone else, like the regents within the infamous University of California school system. However, few persons seem to be outraged in these instances, even when these people are not the best qualified candidates. Many are for certain that if these people were black, folks wouldn't hesitate to be outraged. So what should we make of this? Surely we are not a privileged class nation of hypocrites.

Ironically, some of the companies who continue to layoff thousands of persons who are working to take care of their families, while corporate profits still ride high, have had little widespread criticism aimed at them. Instead, people seem to have focused their attention to other less important issues like affirmative action. The erosion of the middle-class, which affirmative action has little if anything at all to do with, is beyond a doubt, a grave threat to the continued stability of our government, and our country, far more than affirmative action could ever hope to be.

Ironically, however, this appears to be overlooked, in favor of combatting of all things, affirmative action. Give me a break. What ever happened to focusing on the *root causes* of problems?

Walking In The Shoes Of Blacks

I am reminded by a magazine poll that I recently heard on the radio one day, while I was driving. The poll asked if the person polled would favor affirmative action for racial minorities? The overwhelming response was no. But when the poll asked would the individual favor affirmative action for women? The overwhelming response was a resounding yes. Many people wonder, and others are only too sure as to what this is saying about the real attitudes of most affirmative action opponents. What do you think?

Regardless to your opinion, such events obviously suggest that we are not yet a color-blind society, despite wishful thinking. Take for example the criminal justice system. One in three blacks are involved in the criminal justice system in America. In other words, though only 12% of the population, blacks now comprise the majority of prisoners. In fact, our nation has more people in prison, than any other nation on Earth, including the infamous South Africa. But how can this be when blacks only make up 12% of the population? Easy. Take for example our drug laws. If an individual is caught with a mere 5 grams of crack cocaine, the drug of choice by many black drug-users, the penalty is so stiff that an individual must be caught with 500 grams (100 times the amount) of powdered cocaine, the drug of choice for most white drug-users, just to equal the same sentence.

As of 1994, more than 90% of all federal crack cocaine drug offenders were black, as most powder cocaine offenders are usually white, and are plea-bargained. As such, because of sentencing disparities, the result is that far fewer whites are sentenced to long prison terms on drug offenses. And as the money of white parents often buys their children out of the criminal justice system, unlike many poor blacks who do not have the resources, I'm sure you can see how this has created a problem. I'm also sure that you've heard about this debate on television.

So, as you can see, such a situation is only one of many on how so many African-Americans can be unfairly caught up in the legal system, instead of working, and paying taxes. But of course, I guess we shouldn't be surprised that the biggest proponents of such a drug law are from Florida either. Does anyone smell a rat?

And by the way, while we might forget, what is the premise for our criminal system, anyway? Punishment or reforming? My reason for asking is because while some people like to vilify those who are caught committing crimes, no matter how petty, and punish them severely, this obviously does nothing to reform people. And again, this instead of these same people working and paying taxes, hello!

So why is this so? And if punishing crime were the objective, then why are sentences for white-collar crimes so light? Why do statistics show blacks receiving significantly stiffer sentences when committing crimes against whites, than committing crimes against other blacks? Is there not a hidden message being sent here? And surely, this is an accidental oversight, right?

You see, such circumstances are but a couple of many harsh reminders that African-Americans must face everyday, reminding blacks that *race does matter*. In fact, some American Blacks are so conditioned to this type of treatment, that many blacks have just closed their eyes, and have tried to convince themselves that what they have been realizing, really isn't real, but it is.

So as such, many African-Americans are beginning to react accordingly, and unless *companies* respond favorably, such reactions will not be good for most major companies with large black consumer patronage. But as many companies themselves do not currently realize that they even have large amounts of black consumer patronage, such a measure could be disastrous to many who don't even see it coming. Thus, we must begin to adopt one basic principle, "Make no decisions where there is no compassion." For if we do not take a proactive stand regarding such issues, many will likely come to regret their non-progressive actions or non-actions.

A Personal Experience With Affirmative Action

I am reminded of a personal experience with affirmative action while formerly working for a large, prestigious general market ad agency. As I formerly handled much of the advertising for a very large corporation, I also produced and ran ads which often stated things like, "We want to do business with minority businesses."

The reality was, however, that after leaving my former agency to form my own, and after going to my former corporate client for business, I learned that yes, my former client said they wanted to do business with minorities, but the reality was something different.

It turned-out that the company advertised that it wished to do business with qualified minority vendors, showing pictures of black people receiving contracts. However, once qualified minorities actually began to show up on their doorstep, ironically, most minority contracts were quickly awarded to firms owned by white women. And the remainder were mostly awarded to old time friends and college buddies of the mostly white men and women who awarded the contracts--and yes, the recipients of these contracts worth hundreds of thousands and even millions of dollars, were all white. And this is only one of at least a dozen of such stories I could tell.

Another is when I was invited to bid on a local government project, only after some pressure was applied to have more than just major white companies automatically selected as was usually the case. My firm created a "winning masterpiece" in terms of creative works, but the government official in charge of the presentation, unknown to my agency at that time, was on the board of directors of the questionable "firm" who ultimately was awarded the business, despite that "firm" not necessarily presenting the best works, nor it being an ad agency. And needless to say, this was perhaps beyond a conflict of interest.

I'll leave that discussion at that, but this is just to state that these types of incidents are not just a few isolated cases. It happens everyday in our country, on a wide scale, so we are only kidding ourselves with the myths we currently have about affirmative action, because this author can personally tell you that many firms, and government officials, with the federal government being the most progressive, are basically doing what they want to do, period, end of discussion.

So believe me, no one dislikes hearing the words racism or discrimination every time something doesn't go a person's way more than this author. However, after witnessing grossly illogical, unfair and often highly questionable situations, time and time again, sometimes, one must simply accept the premise that if the shoe fits, wear it.

Being from the South, my parents always taught me to: observe, be a man, call a rabbit a rabbit, and a spade a spade. So as such, that is simply what I do.

Now, from the examples above, one might quickly conclude that there was/is an obvious problem at these organizations, but the reality is that if one looks around, then one would quickly conclude that these organizations are no exception, but are the rule--north, south, east, west, the geographic location really does not matter.

The author has known several African-Americans who left one geographic location to escape discrimination, prejudice and racism, and gain opportunities somewhere else. And for some, relocating worked. But for the majority, wherever they seemed to go, prejudice and discrimination seemed to follow them, despite being qualified. I even know of people who for years, literally looked for decent jobs, despite having years of experience and college degrees.

I also met one gentleman who was forced to work for $6 per hour, despite having a master's degree from a "good" school, being remarkably intelligent, and having more than a decade of television and film experience. Now, as this personally made me both sad and angry, all at the same time, and as this may be the case with many other people today, the difference is that this gentleman experienced such hardships long before corporate cutbacks even began. And yes, he is black.

I will sum it up this way. I will disseminate to you an interesting conversation that a friend who has lived both in the north and south, relayed to me. I asked him, from his experience, did he feel that there was a noticeable difference living in the south, compared to living in the north. He said yes, and summed it up this way. "In the north, a black man can basically make as much money as he can make, with few hindrances. White people just don't want blacks living next door. But in the south," he said, white people don't necessarily mind that you (a black person) live next door, as long as you don't make too much money." Perhaps this is the best way to sum up the reality between blacks and whites.

So, functioning normally and competitively within an environment which is both hostile inwardly and on the exterior, is almost inconceivable, and is anything but fair. So perhaps the name misrepresents the reality. Perhaps the words affirmative action should be re-named to "affirmative intentions," which have hardly decimated our society.

One other noteworthy point, however, is that in most instances, when you see black faces in the corporate environment, however few, the majority is usually black females, and not black males. Ever wonder why?

Not All Blacks Are Considered Black

With a background as a public relations professional and motion picture screenwriter, I can tell you that warm and fuzzy stories about businesses doing business with minority businesses are great butter for the press, and sometimes, even the big screen too.

After all, these stories are positive, make corporations look like good corporate citizens, and seem to promote a certain level of utopia. However, in most instances, when companies have alleged minority vendor purchasing policies with 10% goals, the number comparisons do not add up close to 10%. This is especially true with professional services contracts. And in most instances, perhaps you would not be surprised to know that more than half of all so-called minority contract awards are awarded not to racial minority firms, but are awarded to women--many of them affluent and white.

Now, many people are presently lobbying to end "set aside programs," but in the meantime, many of these same people already have access to as much as 90% of all contracts, and are sending wives, daughters, wives of well-to-do friends, etc., to compete for the additional 10%. So blacks, hispanics, asians, other minorities, and white women, all end up fighting over 10%, while few people, including "Angry White Males," challenge those with 90%+, and with 95% of all management-level positions. Does this make sense? Not to this author. Does it make sense to you?

But anyway, adding to an already interesting situation, beginning in the late 1980's, many African-American males, who benefitted from affirmative action, and who later became successful, along with some women, mostly non-black, who also benefitted from affirmative action, suddenly began to argue as many of their white male counterparts. They argued that affirmative action needed to be done away with. These people often argue that affirmative action is a crutch for blacks that blacks don't need. And often times, so-called ultra-conservative blacks with this viewpoint, are put out front to make cases against such measures, even though African-Americans as a group, continue to reside at the bottom of the totem pole in many key socio-economic categories.

There obviously are still very few African-American corporate executives of white-dominated institutions, and substantially fewer African-American *male* corporate executives. But not having African-American executives, plural, not singular, can be more of a detriment for most companies than can be seen at first glance. Nonetheless, however, this phenomenon continues, despite the fact that more African-Americans are college-educated, have valuable experience and/or master's degrees than ever before.

But it should be noted that many successful black females, especially, those whom have sons who will be men one day, feeling that something just isn't right with this picture, are finally beginning to question this syndrome, asking, "Why don't I see very many black males in the corporate environment? I saw them at college, why not here?"

This is what is meant sometimes when people say that no one but a black man, who has had regular experiences of being a black man, (unlike Clarence Thomas types who we know surely have never been discriminated against), can really understand the emotional plight of being a black man, often times, not even a black woman.

But in relating back to why so many African-American males in particular, would stand against affirmative action, and be instrumental in removing it from the system, this must be discussed further. Maybe they know something that the rest of us don't know. But first, let's take a look at the profile of who most affirmative action opponents are.

Aside from a predominant number of white, male Republicans, beer drinking blue-collar workers included, and some well-to-do, Republican white females, who likely benefitted from affirmative action, or at least benefitted from inherited family wealth, the opponents are also largely African-American males who have since become "successful," with good jobs, at least good jobs for right now.

Often times, many of these men are very interested in what their white male counterparts think about them. These men often have lots of white colleagues, and often do not necessarily deliver their heart and soul opinions on issues. However, usually, because of self-serving reasons, this group of men traditionally has chosen to gain the face-value acceptance of their influential white male colleagues, therefore forsaking all others in socio-economic positions they were once in themselves. Thus, these people usually oppose "continued" affirmative action, no matter how great the need, or whatever the cost of its abolition might be.

If one were to research the record of many African-American males who have been appointed to positions of high status, you would quickly learn that traditionally, as few, if not fewer African-Americans, have been promoted, or have benefitted, than if a white male had been doing the hiring, issuing the promotions, or whatever. This syndrome appears to be a little less unfavorable when looking at black female executives, however, who often are not as afraid to make such decisions, and I'm speaking from personal experience.

You see, unfortunately, usually, many African-Americans, upon walking through the door of opportunity, often strangely close that door behind them. They do this to feel less threatened, have less "competition" in their world, and to feel that they have achieved a pinnacle that other blacks were not able to accomplish but them. Other times, many are intimidated, and are often fearful of being singled-out if they hire one too many blacks in their bosses eyes, and in many cases, one can be too many, so regardless, these people often do not hire other blacks.

And blacks are also sometimes exploited by well-to-do blacks, who choose to "be black," only when it's convenient, and benefits them. These persons often live in small mansions, and drive excessively expensive automobiles, but pay their workers low wages, provide them with no health insurance, and no future.

Are these people any different from white companies who exploit blacks? No. Should these persons or companies be dealt with in the same manner as exploitative white-owned companies? Yes. The bottom line is that it does not matter what color the person is who does the exploiting of black people, it cannot be tolerated, period. This is what is meant by the phrase, "black people's saviour is not in fostering limited individual wealth." If that wealth is gained by the wrong, unprogressive individual, who would people really be helping?

If one looks even more closely, you will probably find that the African-American male or female power broker you see, seemingly no matter how big or small, 98% of the time, must answer ultimately to a white male-- either as a client or boss, directly or indirectly. So, for right now, the question persists, who really has the power to change? These types of instances clearly illustrate that the concept "powerless in a suit" is alive and well now, more than ever.

But regardless, as many anti-affirmative action blacks' motivations are self-motivated, these persons are seen as an abomination. Though ironically, after the dust clears, usually, no one on either side respects these people.

Some companies, which after having a better understanding of the plight of African-Americans, and after understanding that not all blacks are considered black by blacks, will be sensitive to such issues facing this market, and will be true leaders into the 21st Century. And then again, some will not. But nonetheless, the successful companies will most likely be those companies who have attempted to position themselves nicely within the African-American segment, because its the right thing to do, not necessarily just because of profits.

For those few companies which take such stands, and who have taken the time necessary to understand, be sensitized to, and perhaps empathize with issues related to African-Americans, and do the right thing, for those who believe in good being rewarded, instead of greed or evil, the long-term rewards will likely prove fruitful in many ways. However, such corporate involvement must still be gauged and at least, "down-sized," not only by Black America, but America as a whole.

The reason is because regardless, Corporate America mustn't be so intertwined with America that it becomes a group of powerful, elite tyrants which control the political process, and are uncontrollable, especially now that the Corporate Cut Throat Trend is in play. And with regard to Black America, it should down-size its dependence so black people will not be "contributed to" right out of power, and lose their voices for the sake of integration. What should be done in the meantime? Scale back unnecessary luxuries, quit building houses on sand, and begin to construct a steel framed house on solid ground which can withstand the test of time, hopefully for one's children to enjoy.

Dr. King even talked of this fact, and the possibility of a temporary black withdrawal, when in 1967 in Miami, he said, "There may be a temporary way station on the way to an integrated society," and "I do not want to be integrated out of power." Such feelings are often not discussed, however, as even though Dr. King was once literally hated by millions of whites, many whites today have chosen to adopt his memory as a kinder, gentler, non-threatening person, as many today are still fighting for what Dr. King died for.

So black prominence will not be easy, nor necessarily ever come, as long as blacks are dependent upon, and seek to make their money from corporations. In fact, I am not even sure that this should continue at all, especially when you have a $300 billion pot of your own. Blacks must become self-supportive--virtually every other ethnic group has. Remember my selling your soul to the Devil analogy? Are there ever any extenuating circumstances when one should sell his or her soul to the Devil? Is not the price always too high? And remember, one can't get just a little bit pregnant, so simply consider this for what it's worth.

However, from a progressive, "sensitive corporation" perspective, assuming that such corporate bodies still exist, somewhere, improper methodology may still cause companies to miss the mark, as many times, companies usually simply hire one African-American to oversee purchasing from minority vendors, minority recruitment, or whatever. Often times, companies expect this one for all approach to somehow improve the sales and public relations for their companies. And sometimes, it might. But, as it may be of no surprise, despite how noble such intentions might be, these intentions often have a crucial flaw--the individual.

For an example, look no further than to Justice Clarence Thomas--a man who often times goes *harshly* against blacks, as notable and well-respected former federal Judge and Harvard Law Professor, Leon Higginbotham pointed out. This is often the case even when seven white justices, including conservatives, deliver 7-2 decisions, in favor of clearly abused, black victim's cases.

Perhaps Justice Thomas should be considered as a noteworthy example of victims with racial and complexion self-hatred, as the analysis may suggest.

One cannot necessarily tell by looking, but many such individuals exist, and would hardly increase public relations and the like, for most companies. In fact, the reverse may even often be the case, because many of these people are out-of-touch with the marketplace they would be in charge of reaching. And just think, a person with an attitude such as Clarence Thomas once oversaw the Equal Employment Opportunity Commission?

So, this is why this one-for-all solution just does not work without at least some rigorous checks and balances.

Let's turn the tables for a moment. If you were forced to operate under the laws of black men, which were written by black men, for black men, and black men controlled virtually every facet of the society in which you lived, outnumbering you nearly six to one, would that be an uncomfortable scenario to you?

Wouldn't you feel perhaps as many African-Americans feel about the parallel situation which they must face? So again, try to make no decisions where there is no compassion.

Summation

In the past, white men regularly told black men, "Instead of sitting and screaming discrimination, try to find yourselves other opportunities. This is America, and the opportunities exist, if you're not shiftless and lazy, and are willing to work hard to find them. This should be the case as opposed to screaming discrimination." The harsh irony of these words can serve as being very symbolic. And I'm sure that many fifty year-old, recently fired, once $50,000+ earning corporate managers, engineers, and scientists, who once may have felt this way themselves, can now agree.

Even U.S. automobile executives screamed discriminatory foul when Japan refused to make Japanese markets as open to U.S. automobile makers as American markets are open to Japanese products.

So as one can see, this land should not be about winner takes all, but should be about opportunities, fairness, and a decent life for us all, or certainly as many as possible--wouldn't you agree? However, as talk backed by little action often seems to be the remedy, this can afford to be the case no longer. Time has run out.

A belief which is rapidly becoming more prevalent, is the belief that America can operate tactfully, without government involvement. And this belief can *certainly* be appreciated by this author. However, on the other hand, and unfortunately, history has shown us that in a capitalistic society such as ours, we cannot be expected to regulate ourselves. In fact, even state governments cannot adequately do the trick.

A recent computerized study performed by the *Wall Street Journal*, indicated that home-loan approvals to blacks increased by more than 38% from 1993 to 1994, and loans to hispanics rose by 31% during the same time period. This favorable happening, however, appears to have only been caused because of tougher fair-lending enforcement and federal community-investment rules, which have encouraged such loans and required public disclosure of every mortgage lender's loans by race and income.

So, this example is only one to show that under our system of government, governmental involvement is unfortunately, often necessary, especially when money is involved. For if Congress has not passed a law declaring a particular activity illegal, even though it may be totally, morally, and despicably wrong, unfortunately, individuals often tend to act like little children in a candy store, gorging everything they can for monetary gain.

And with the size of some companies these days, if the government is not at least larger than them, with the people having at least some representation, who will ever control these companies? Remember my "subtle prediction" about the future turning into a real life science fiction movie, with rich greedy guys and corporations controlling everything?

Just ponder for a moment that without government intervention, we would likely still have at least some form of the horrible slavery institution, larger amounts of insider trading, extinct wild-life, contaminated rivers, lakes and streams, and $5 per day wages, because of irresponsible, money-hungry corporations. This is unfortunately the people that Americans have come to be, or perhaps, even more scarier to ponder, the people that Americans have always been.

So, Americans must learn to move along together, and fairly, and rid ourselves of rich, elitist tyrants. For if we do not, and if the people allow some of our wild congressional leaders and others to persist with such negative attacks, then eventually, business *will suffer*, and we as Americans can literally watch our clocks until our nation's demise--a situation where we would *all* lose.

A New Age of Blacks In America

Despite negative connotations and stereotypes historically being associated with blacks, nearly every black with whom the author has had contact with in the last two years, those who have been forty years of age or under, has had a college degree. And of the others who didn't have degrees, most were extremely close to having a degree. This is phenomenal, as this has all seemed to really happen just within the last 10-15 years.

This was not the case with previous black generations. In most instances, this was just the opposite. But many of today's blacks are indeed a new breed, and they demand the respect they deserve. Realizing that many of the generations before them were greatly oppressed, and did not have such opportunities, today's generation was once told that education was the key to their success.

So as such, these people, finally able to smell the scent of success, came out of college, were ready for the world, and were then greeted with yet more challenges. It seemed that each time blacks would jump through one hoop, another would be added, steadily and persistently keeping them from, as Dr. King called it, "the prize."

This is so as many of today's younger blacks have been greeted with "Oh, I'm sorry, but we're cutting back," or "We're on a hiring freeze...," or "Okay, Republicans are in office, great. Sorry fella, but we've met our quota, thanks anyway," or even, "I'm sorry, but you're over qualified."

Now, with such disappointments have come a rush of young, talented, aggressive blacks, many with a great entrepreneurial spirit, and something to prove. Many are tired of waiting, and having yet another obstacle to cross to escape the clutches of poverty. And just when an overwhelming number of blacks are attempting to operate successfully within the confines of the system, suddenly, something else seems to be blocking their paths, or another hoop has been added.

As it has come to be known in the black community, blacks are sick and tired of the white man's tricks with no treat. So as such, many courageous blacks have begun to focus on entrepreneurial activities, rather than choosing to reside within the traditional corporate "mainstream," which often seems to stifle, oppress them, and/or utterly reject them, both professionally and socially.

So with a whole host of college-educated blacks, blacks are now saying, "In the past, we just gave away $300 billion to white-owned companies without even so much as a thank you." But that has changed, and the new age of blacks are saying this must change. Low levels of employment, low wage paying jobs, no health insurance...These are things that blacks are all too familiar with, and many have finally grown tired, once and for all.

Quite frankly, though operating with meager resources, today, aggressive young black men and women from across the country are getting creative, and have, using a phrase from urban black youngsters, "come stomping into the '90's."

The Irony Of Struggles

Until the political climate is perceived to be more hospitable, and on a fairer playing field for blacks, then many African-Americans will do as many are doing now, seeking-out other non-traditional ways for themselves, as they reassess the situation.

Look around you. Notice that no longer will you see as many of today's blacks "shucking and jiving," and hanging out in clubs as in years past. In fact, many of today's blacks have grown quite serious, and the amount of intelligence one would find even on street corners now-a-days', is astonishing. Much more focused attention is realized today than in years past.

Blacks will likely soon come to slow down their buying from companies which sell tremendous volumes of products to blacks, but which have few African-Americans working for its company, few in important, management-level, decision-making positions, and even fewer business contracts with black companies. After all, blacks feel that most whites do not buy from black-owned companies, so why should blacks continue to buy from white-owned companies which do not even treat them with respect? This attitude is catching-on across the country, and in a short period of time, this will likely finally begin to prompt many changes which should have been made long ago.

Many young blacks will likely become successful beyond their own expectations of success, despite often being turned down for employment and other opportunities.

Many will likely use their creative energies, and do as many successful blacks have done already--start their own businesses, and startle themselves even with their own successes. And remember, overnight success usually takes about 10 years.

Do you remember my informing you a few chapters ago about the New York ethnic advertising giant, Uniworld? Well, years ago, the company's founder, Byron Lewis, being a young, smart, creative, and aggressive black man, attempted to get a job with more than 30 advertising agencies in New York. He was turned down by each and every one. However, today, since then, Lewis opened his own agency, and after several years in the business, and after some struggles, today, his firm now bills-out more than $100 million annually--the irony of struggles.

But Lewis is just one of many such pioneers, Sam Chisholm of the Mingo group, Caroline Jones, famous for the adage, "Strong enough for a man, but made for a woman," Tom Burrell, the trio of Muse, Cordero, Chen, and others. And these are just successful pioneers within the long-time closed-off to blacks, advertising agency arena. So as there are many others, in literally hundreds of professions, my point is that most successful blacks were virtually "forced" into success by "mainstream," white resistance, and undoubtedly, these people won't be the last of such bitter-sweet success stories.

An Important Real Life Story

Let me share with you the real deal, in a real life story. I will share with you the story of George Johnson, a successful African-American businessman from Chicago, IL, who founded Johnson Hair Products in the late 1960's.

Being no relation to *Jet Magazine* publisher, John H. Johnson, after working for a company for many years, George Johnson attempted to obtain a $700 bank loan from a bank in which he had a good standing.

Mr. Johnson told his loan officer that the loan would be used by him to open up his own business. The loan officer smiled at him, went away, and eventually came back stating that the loan was denied.

A few days later, Mr. Johnson applied again, with the same bank, but at a different branch. He stated to the white loan officer that he wanted to take his wife on a vacation with the $700 loan request. In approximately one hour, the loan officer stated that the loan was approved.

The moral to this story? Blacks often can get loans to purchase cars, go on vacation, etc. In other words, they can get loans to spend money. But when blacks seek to get loans to start their own businesses, and one day sustain economic clout, they usually encounter massive negative resistance from banks. Should this tell us anything?

So again, as I informed you earlier, in a tough economy, the African-American market is one of the few groups which will keep the economy moving along, however slightly, with its continued, vast purchases, even despite rough economic outlooks. So undoubtedly, the African-American market is where great battles will be won or lost. And as a direct spin-off from this market, numerous other groups will likely join or follow. So, what I am stating is that for many companies deemed as "exploitative," now couldn't be a better time to change that image, hint, hint.

The point? If companies wish to prosper in the future, they perhaps would be wise to start poising themselves for future business opportunities, shedding yesterday's thinking, and beginning to show fairness while it is still even remotely interesting to blacks. In fact, I would advise my clients that this should happen right away.

The Value Of Black Dollars

As I have informed you already that many companies have wrongly perceived the black market to be non-essential, or of less value than it really is, then allow me to illustrate my point with one shining example.

Remember the dramatic impact of the Montgomery, Alabama Civil Rights Bus Boycott--you know, the one started by Rosa Parks and Dr. Martin Luther King, Jr., challenging the unjust treatment of Jim Crow segregationist laws?

Well, my point is that the bus company did not seek to end the boycott because their hearts softened, or because racism began to disappear. Hardly was the case in either of these instances. Aside from the Supreme Court, the bus company primarily changed its policies largely because of the economic impact of blacks not riding the bus. For blacks had come to decide that it was far better to walk with dignity, than to ride in shame. Why it was perhaps Black America's finest hour, and this courageous, glorified intolerance on the part of blacks, proved to be very devastating to that company's bottom line, and beneficial to blacks everywhere. I hope companies will not have to experience things like this before favorable actions are taken in the future, although the author is not necessarily optimistic in this regard.

You see, what many do not understand is that many of today's blacks are quite wealthy, regardless to any old perceptions which might have once existed.

Just like anything else, while not all, many black families have evolved from people with very little, to advancing to people with dozens of companies worth tens of millions of dollars. There is indeed a difference between blacks of today, and blacks thirty years ago.

So, with this evolutionary process, many companies have not kept pace with the black market. Instead, companies continue to operate with assumptions based upon situations from thirty years ago, and this will undoubtedly negatively affect these organizations.

In case you still don't understand, quite simply, the new generation of blacks has grown tired and weary of being taken for granted by companies and politicians. These people have realized that blacks were mistreated for years, even though many disputed, and still dispute their claims today. So, as blacks are beginning to realize that they cannot depend on others to help them carry-out the dream of Dr. Martin Luther King, a black economic preservation/revolution sentiment is growing deeper and deeper, especially among younger, educated blacks. Some call it "Black Nationalism," but regardless to what you call it, as Dr. Cornel West states, "as long as black people are viewed as a 'them' when problems are involved such as crime, violence and poverty, and an 'us' only when certain issues appear to be on the horizon, then 'Black Nationalism' will thrive."

Most of today's African-Americans would like nothing better than to be able to move along in harmony with whites. But with history as their teacher, and decades after an alleged warmer, more socially hospitable America, as Dr. West also states, "blacks are tired of seemingly having to do all of the cultural and moral work necessary for healthy race relations. This in essence, suggests that only certain Americans can define what it means to truly be an American, while everyone else just must fit-in." This pompous set of beliefs obviously will no longer continue to work either.

As long as double standards continue between whites and others, this sentiment will continue to grow and multiply. Do you still dispute claims of white double standards? If so, then look no further than to your nearest idea box (your television set), and begin to count how many white men you find being intimate with black women, compared to how many black men you find doing the same with white women--Does this have any significance? You bet your last dollar it does, and I don't think I have to explain why.

You see, in the past, many blacks virtually bent over backwards to "get along with whites," and participate in activities with whites. As such, many whites were flattered that so many blacks wanted something that whites had. But like a classic case of normal human psychology, this became an ego boost. The result? Also like a classic ego boosting case, many whites began to feel more arrogant and pride-filled. So harmony prevailed, but when times began to get tough, and problems followed, the concept of "us" quickly turned to "them" and "they" by most whites. The dream of Dr. Martin Luther King seemed to begin to disappear into the shadows, as whites rapidly began exclusively driving on the freeways, by-passing neglected inner cities, moving into the suburbs, and withdrawing their children from schools with large black populations--"White Flight" as it has come to be called.

Feeling betrayed, abandoned, and backlashed by most whites, many blacks feel that if they cannot purchase products and services from black-owned businesses, they would prefer to go without. But hold-on, we are not talking poor, uneducated blacks, or people on welfare, we are talking about the market in which companies would least like to give up, the much liberal-spending, educated, black middle-class. And these attitudes are growing widely, and everyday, as more blacks, regardless of their career and educational attainments, seem to be given daily reminders and more incentives to do away with the dreams of Dr. King and his concept of "fair integration."

So responsible businesses obviously have more than just a responsibility here. And as blacks appreciate doing business where there is adequate black representation, prominence, acceptance, and respect, what's wrong with that?

This is why it is so crucial that for companies who wish to thrive beyond the competition, by all means, they should not lose their black customers. After all, African-Americans have legitimate complaints, and the compassion and fairness they seek is not asking too much.

But hold in mind that we are not talking about charity, because for those companies and organizations who give these things, there will likely be rich rewards waiting in the wings. But for those who do not, these companies undoubtedly will soon come to regret their non-efforts, patronizing efforts, or lack of efforts.

But hold on, there is still yet another reason for major overhauls by most companies. If our present social climate persists, and as many of our current politicians seem unwilling to do anything constructive about the present situation, then businesses must act. Why? Because if any type of uneasiness continues as a result of what has been brewing for quite some time now, then businesses *will* suffer.

This is why businesses must utilize their efficient means of action, as opposed to waiting for our Congress to take a "long way around the barn" type of approach to implementing fairness and solutions. Business must take a leadership role, which can perhaps serve to be as effective as any marketing or public relations efforts one has ever tried. And at the same time, such actions might really add some valued credibility to one's company. For instance, when Sam Walton, the founder of Wal-Mart was living, America loved him. Why? Because he was a billionaire who wore clothes from Wal-Mart, he drove a 1972 Chevrolet pickup truck, and was non-pretentious. In essence, he captured the ideals of many middle-class Americans, and hence built a loyal, very profitable market. Hint, hint, this is at least something to consider. But nonetheless, if the U.S. is to again become a leading power, then undoubtedly, large numbers of citizens will too have to become involved in this revolutionary process.

Let's Talk Politics

Business Is Politics

By now, it's no great secret that most politicians serve as legal prostitutes. In fact, virtually each time we elect someone to Congress, the Senate, or whatever, no matter how good their initial intentions to change a broken system, ultimately, we end up electing a legal prostitute. These are strong words, I know, but you show me one person who disagrees, and I'll show you a politician.

Regardless to what politicians might think, their jobs are to carry-out the wishes of those who got them where they are--And in higher offices, especially, in most cases, that's big business.

But anyway, often times, the way the game is currently played, politicians vote yes or no on behalf of the highest bidder--it's that simple. That's the game of politics. And when you as a congressman/woman are forced to raise at least $5,000 for every week while you're in office, just to be able to make the next race, what do you think ultimately takes precedence? That's right, money first. Business of the people second, or even third, or maybe fourth.

Make no mistake about it, in many instances, politics, crime, and business are all one in the same--they're well, just packaged a little bit differently. In fact, the only significant difference between these three, is that only in politics, nothing happens by chance.

If people are wondering why we currently have grid-lock in Washington, why the rich is getting richer, the poor getting poorer, Medicare being cut, and tax breaks for the wealthy, the answer is this... In general, since Republicans have been labeled as the party of trickle-down economics and pro-big business, should anyone be surprised that big business will contribute large amounts to politicians to ensure that their business' interests are looked after?

Once money changes hands, an obligation then results, and whether they like it or not, the politician must vote the way his or her large contributor wishes for him or her to vote, and usually, he or she does. Why? Because to vote against such powerful interests means all sorts of things, including the fact that one likely will not have enough money to run in the future, because such a large contributor has pulled-out. This is the real world, apart from fiction.

Maybe this situation could become worse, however. Maybe that once large contributor is now suddenly giving money to that politician's biggest opponent. Thus, we have increased premiums to Medicare recipients, tax breaks for the wealthy, etcetera, etcetera. And with the middle-class consistently being eroded, many of our rich elite are in a since, ridding themselves of any competition or "threats," because if these people have anything to do with it, no one else will have any money to contribute. The wealthy stick together, because these individuals all have something in common, keeping their money! The rest of us are fractionalized by design-- over affirmative action, abortion, and the like. This guarantees victory for some. So, eventually, at the rate we are traveling, "common persons" will come to be at the mercy of our rich elite. Does that sound like the makings of a democracy to you?

During elections, people will do and say virtually anything to get into office. But it's usually not until after they get into office that they worry about solving a problem, or worst, find out how places like Washington really work. "Here's money for your vote," or "No vote, no money," and with the kinds of dollars I told you one must raise, small businesses and the average citizen do not stand a chance. And this is how our future will turn even nastier.

Frankly, when the average voter goes to the polls today, he or she is going to get screwed. But in essence, people simply vote to elect the person who will screw them the least. So after such an evaluation, one must then pose the question, is our system the root of today's problems? My answer to you is both yes and no.

The Root Of Our Political Problems

While the system does have its flaws, we must remember that such a system has survived splendidly over centuries. So surely, the system by itself cannot be our problem. But on the other hand, we must also remember that we are using a system based upon principles, beliefs, and the size of companies, from more than 200 years ago. And this system, if it were a business, would have undoubtedly been updated with the times, long ago.

So maybe, just maybe, even with our Constitutional Amendments, we are working with an outdated book of rules. But yet, our problem undoubtedly is with the people within our system too. For the people within our system are often so filled with corruption, special interest groups, paybacks, kickbacks, and favors, it is literally impossible for "the people" to get virtually any fair legislation. Why Washington is a cesspool. We all know that. However, for some unknown reason, we continue to wade in that cesspool. Is that intelligent on our parts?

Remember the days of Julius Caesar and Rome? Well, not only with Caesar's home, but with all of the great empires which have ever fallen, virtually all have done so because of political corruption, and internal strife--sound familiar?

Maybe we should not be surprised that we now have the problems in which our society must face. Perhaps we are on a rendezvous with destiny. But regardless, this means that we are likely on our way to becoming a society that becomes separated by those who have experienced the ills of the system, versus those who have not. And unfortunately/fortunately, many people today have begun to feel the ills once only felt by blacks, hispanics, and American Indians. But regardless, the real tragedy is that a large portion of our problems were voted in by the very people who are being hurt today. Maybe this should tell us something.

Will More Black Leaders Help?

One intellectual question which has persisted over the last several years has been, will more black leaders help the situation of under-represented people such as blacks? Many believe that more black leaders will help America cure some of the problems facing common people. However, black leadership does not necessarily constitute black politicians. With previous generations of blacks desperately wishing to obtain the ways and lifestyles of whites, like the Cherokee Indians of the mid-1800's, seeking individual wealth, they often developed the same attitudes and mind-sets of whites, prompting many successful blacks to act not much different than whites, though they are often still treated differently.

Under our current system, the new generation of black leadership will hinge upon black leaders who are not necessarily politicians. For sometimes, politicians can be too easily controlled by outside influences, such as corporations. As such, blacks must work with what works best for blacks, and that is not necessarily the current "mainstream way" of doing things.

However, blacks must take at least one page from the playbook of whites. Historically, when something has not worked to the advantage of whites, whites have fought fiercely to change the rules of the game. The new generation of blacks, and now others, undoubtedly will and must accept this call-to-action.

But getting back on track, with regard to politics, as it stands currently, if there is not the numerical strength available to pass or stop certain legislation in our system, then black politicians in particular, would then generally be better served by "going along with the flow," and not "creating any waves," the kind of black person whom I describe as usually being "liked" by most whites. But when the dust settles, to be liked is fine, but to be respected is a far more noteworthy achievement.

For the sake of argument, assuming that black politicians could be a savior for disadvantaged persons, also naively assumes that black politicians will be unlike white politicians, and not sell themselves to the highest bidder, as historically, many politicians have done. Why? Because often times, people are wrapped into excessive individual achievements, and excessive materialism, both of which often cause persons to lose their better judgement, thus sell their souls to the Devil for a few years of prosperity.

Many years after his death, the name Malcolm X was often taboo for many blacks and obviously for whites. The reason? White society seemed to ostracize any blacks who identified with this man's teachings. And this intimidation continues through today, meaning the early 1990's, a time in which until then, many blacks surprisingly, knew little about Malcolm X. This was realized through some research in which I initiated beginning in 1990. The mere mention of his name, even in black households, was spoken with sheer reluctance. And often, even black politicians distanced themselves from this man. Remember, when you've got your hands in corporate back pockets, you are bound not to rock the boat.

In one of my own personal encounters, a young lady I had happened to be dating at the time, shrieked when I told her that we would be watching Spike Lee's Malcolm X movie on the VCR one evening. Her immediate reply to me was "I don't want to watch that kind of movie." Obviously curious, I asked her what did she mean by "that kind of movie," she replied "...that junk."

This young lady, by the way, was a very bright, intelligent black woman, who changed her mind upon viewing the movie. As a matter of fact, she's my wife today. However, back then, she knew very little about Malcolm X, and the little that she did know was certainly negative and prejudicial. Where did she learn such attitudes? The media? School...?

You see, in the past, blacks often simply took what they were taught at face-value, and simply believed what they were told. But my staunch warning to you today is that finally, this face-value acceptance has begun to disappear, and is treated with suspicion by most people, especially those who know that they have been "burned" before.

Contrasting Martin Luther King, Jr. And Malcolm X

Most people have been indoctrinated to believe that Malcolm X was some sort of evil doer and Dr. Martin Luther King was the only true saint. No wonder so many blacks rejected the media's negative picture painted of Minister Louis Farrakhan, and attended and/or supported the Million Man March. Despite blasting Louis Farrakhan, many of these same critics hardly uttered a word about Newt Gingrich, Pat Buchanan, and others, or their beliefs and teachings.

So in noticing these types of things, the media-instilled, nasty, rebel-like images of Malcolm X and others, have been virtually washed away in the minds of many people, both black and white, and especially, those persons under age thirty. The reason? Because much or all of what these leaders once said, appears to be shining true today.

Isn't it ironic that so many whites "love" Dr. King today? Many forget, however, that certainly was not the case while he was living though.

During those times, like today, if Malcolm X could have been bought or controlled by the white-male dominated establishment, he would have been. He, however, made it very clear to all that he would not be bought, in any form or fashion. As such, he posed an obvious threat to those who had benefitted, and continue to benefit from an unGodly system.

The memory of Dr. King at least, is that he was more of a gradual motivator, a non-violent believer. Though he was respected, because of his one-sided portrayal, and "non-threatening" image adopted by the white establishment, some call him a white man's champion, advocating non-violence against even those who were out to have themselves some "fun" on the backs of pick-up trucks, taunting, lynching and carrying-out violence against blacks.

To explain Malcolm X, he believed that if blacks and whites could get along, that would be wonderful. However, he had his suspicions that whites, largely white men, would be unwilling to relinquish any of their great advantages and power, so that black men could equally provide decent lives for them and their families. Thus, he believed that white men in power would continue to try to control blacks through economics. After all, one of the most proven ways to control people has been shown to be through economics. The reason? Because if you hinder someone economically, many other ripple effects will occur. Hence, you have crime and violence, traditional problems with the black family, etcetera, etcetera.

It should be noted that Malcolm X had a strong contrasting belief from Dr. King in that he believed that if whites should attack blacks with violence, blacks being no less human than whites, should by all means, be self-respecting people, and retaliate against their aggressors--in much the same way as Jewish people have believed in Israel, or as the United States believes if she should ever be attacked.

In a nutshell, these are the two basic ideologies, and main differences between these men. Regardless to who was right or wrong regarding these and such issues, if anyone was right or wrong, one strong premise remains-- neither man would have been as effective without the other.

Why Things Have Begun To Change

Because of Malcolm's often vocal, serious threats to those who had been prospering at the expense of blacks, primarily the wealthy white establishment, and because of his obvious commitment and exemplary strong leadership of African-Americans, if he could not be bought to "control his people," he had to be done away with.

It should be no surprise then that Malcolm X would be the first of the two famed civil rights activists to die. For had he survived, and Dr. King been assassinated first, there would have been obvious retaliatory bloodshed on the part of whites in America. Dr. King's obvious non-violence message, as many believe, was the deciding factor that Dr. King could be harmed only after the systematic assassination of Malcolm X.

Any wonders why even today, many large companies praise Dr. King during Black History Month, but very few ever give any recognition to Malcolm X? This demonstrates that the process of control, persuasion and manipulation through mass communications is as powerful today as ever.

Perhaps it should not be shocking to learn that today's educated blacks are turning more Afro-centric, or getting back to their original heritage, than ever before. This, as opposed to continuing to operate exclusively within white society's ideological confines, while leaving behind all consciousness of who they really are.

This, however, has only begun to happen recently. Why? Because before, there were too few blacks in the middle-class to retain their own identity without sanctions being applied from White America--a reason why black businesses and viable organizations must be supported by blacks and their $300 billion. Today,

more blacks are beginning to open their own businesses, substantially more have become educated, many have become used to struggles, and a past of continuing to accept virtual second-class citizenship appears to be intolerable any longer.

So what does this mean? It means that blacks have begun and must continue to take a much larger interest in their own future.

Black Americans have the economic power to change many things in America, but that economic power has traditionally been channeled in many conflicting directions. In the past, Black Americans, for a diverse number of reasons, have preferred to spend their money with white-owned companies, especially older Black Americans. These people purchased and many continue to purchase white produced products, even when black companies produce and sell the same things for the same price, or less expensive. Jewish persons, Asian persons and Italians all have gained acceptance not through social engineering, but through economic and political avenues. Each group has its own distinct and separate identity from the "mainstream," and this has gained these groups acceptance and respect. Perhaps its finally about time for blacks to take a page from this successful historical analysis.

In the past, most blacks, keying-off of the indoctrination by whites, had seemed to have the infamous bad experience of working with blacks. So, they automatically assumed to seek-out someone white, perceiving that their products and services would be of higher quality. The problem with this remedy, however, was that all seemed to forget the infamous bad experience of working with whites.

Don't get me wrong, some blacks did practice being in businesses in which they did not properly train themselves to effectively handle their customer's needs, and this cannot be excused. However, with the wealth of talent and expertise available today, one should not be guilty of overlooking those who are quite adept at handling the needs of their customers, and there are many more of these persons and organizations than one might think. So in other words, "buying black" is a two way street, persons just should be sure that they are not on the wrong street.

And this is also stated to say that blacks should not be so quick to automatically take the position of people who have not walked in their shoes. Blacks also should be cautioned to not criticize or elaborate on issues which they know little about. One's ignorance about a particular subject is not a crime, but can be dangerously misused against that person or others, becoming a very powerful weapon.

So no longer should black people continue to have the old slave mind-set that if a person's skin is black, his or her products will be of less quality. In many cases, because of the Hell in which blacks must go through to be successful, often times, the reverse is true. Many blacks are guilty of this "cardinal sin," but many today are determined to refuse to keep falling prey to it.

But if a black person is not skilled in a particular area, they should stay out of that field, because producing low-quality products will certainly not benefit anyone, but will hurt black people as a whole. So, as consumers, demand the best from black-owned businesses, this will help maintain excellence, which is important to the long-term success of Black America.

In closing this discussion, it should be noted that for right now, African-Americans are continuing to purchase goods and services of exploitative companies. But, if your organization is one of these such companies, black or white, be forewarned that less happy days are much nearer than one might think.

A Home Hitting Example

As an example, just think what would happen if young African-Americans alone decided not to buy the sneakers of a leading sneaker manufacturer for one year. The effects would be disastrous for such a company. Do you think that they would then promote and hire African-Americans by the dozens to correct their little "oversight?" I'd be willing to bet that they would. And to take things a step further, what if, and I do believe that this will soon happen, consumers stopped buying the products of those companies who have begun to fire tens of thousands of employees, simply to make more profits?

As many of these organizations allegedly support family values, yet help destroy the family nucleus, how hypocritical can this be? These sorts of actions undoubtedly will prompt much change in America in the near future, as new generations of both blacks and whites say, "Enough Is Enough!"

When *several*, and several being the operative word, African-Americans work in decision-making capacities for companies, then at least one or more is bound to seek to hire more qualified African-Americans, which inevitably puts pressure on other black executives to hire more blacks also.

However, as long as there is the good ole' token at each company, nothing will get better, because these persons feel obligated to protect their territory and maintain the status-quo. These people feel that they are the elite, privileged person, and they transcend that into serving as "gate keepers" against other blacks with rising star potential.

Blacks have the power to change, but for the last thirty years, have chosen not to use it. However, every indication that this author has seen appears to again say, "No more." The unfortunate token black executives that exist in many white-controlled organizations right now is a joke, though no one is laughing. The reason is because, often times, few if any of these people actually have any true decision-making power without the okay of a white superior. And sadly enough, that's almost always the way that it is. This gives the appearance that America hasn't changed, and that history may again be repeating itself--slave, master and overseer.

But for evil-doers, the Bible gives us a prophecy, "Do not be deceived, God is not mocked; for whatever a man sows, that he will also reap" (Galatians 6:7). I, like many others, have seen this prophecy at work before, many times.

Many people, those who have not been fair or just, are frankly scared to death of this and Biblical verses like these, because of their misdeeds.

As a consequence, many of these people often foolishly attempt to do anything to avert their destinies, not realizing that whatever we reap, we will also sow, and averting such a principle just is not possible. So, my words to all who may fall prey to such a thing is, though we all may "owe" for our sins, it may never be too late to repent, and save our souls.

American Hypocrisy

No matter how we look at it, Americans have historically been highly hypocritical regarding issues of race. But so that people can better understand, we'll start at the beginning to see what I mean.

Take Thomas Jefferson for instance. As one of our nation's founding fathers, and as the man who wrote the famous words, "All men are created equal," describing that every man has certain inalienable rights which others should not trespass, this man owned more than 90 slaves at the time of writing such document.

In fact, the very issue of slavery was discussed while devising the American Constitution, as it was a pro-slavery document. But regardless, for political purposes, it was decided that blacks were "less than human beings," thus it was simply declared law. Laws are necessary to keep law and order in a civilized society. And God himself even delivered laws to us. However, over the centuries, man-made laws have often proven themselves to be evil, and self-serving. Maybe we should not be surprised that so many African-Americans and Latin Americans today are skeptical of "the law?" After all, the law has often times been unfair to these people, and time and time again, "the law" has been finagled to deliver an iron fist to "unprivileged minority groups" in our country. And it took the O.J. Simpson trial for Americans to just now decide that an overhaul of our justice system is needed?

But getting back to Thomas Jefferson, some historians today wish to quickly excuse him for participating in such evil practices as slavery. They often state that he only did various things, because it was simply the way of the time period in which he lived.

That's interesting, considering that he has been labeled an intellectual, and even children know right from wrong. I hear the arguments of pro-Jefferson supporters, who often say "he only did it because of the time period in which he lived," but assuming that there is a God in heaven, I wonder how that argument will weigh to he who must judge us all?

Many youngsters today are selling drugs, does that mean that they should be excused because it's the "norm" of the period in which they live too?

In all fairness to Jefferson, it is often stated in history books that Jefferson abhorred slavery. But what is often not stated, however, is that Jefferson owned slaves all of his life, and unlike George Washington, never freed his.

But still, relating to Thomas Jefferson as a basic model for our parallel American society example, he was also a very outspoken, leading spokesperson against the issue of race-mixing. He often stated that he could not imagine black men and women living on terms of social equality with whites. He even talked at times of resettling all blacks in some distant land, which might sound familiar today.

But it has since surfaced, despite his negative attitude toward blacks, that Jefferson fathered several black children by one of his black slaves, Sally Hemings, who began having Jefferson's children at the tender age of 14. With Hemings, it appeared that Jefferson had a great fascination, but under today's laws, frankly, Jefferson would have been considered a criminal, at least if Hemings was white.

This scenario reminds me of the words of one of my professors years ago. "There are no such things as great men. There are only men who do great things." There perhaps has never been words spoken which carries more truth.

Picture something for a moment. Each year, African-Americans continue to spend billions of dollars, often surpassing the amounts spent by whites on various consumer items. Yet, despite our feelings of progress, even though there has been some, already, that progress has become greatly threatened. So frankly and candidly, the only real difference between America of today, and America of yester-year, seems to be that today, thanks to corporate greed, we are all now vulnerable to being without, it's no longer just "a black thing." So as such, how much longer do you reasonably believe that such a trend will last before people begin to negatively respond to rich, greedy tyrants, and a rich, greedy Corporate America? Judging from big picture current events, I'd say not long.

Justice Or Politics?

Our land's most elite court, the Supreme Court, is a very powerful body. However, I wish for us to consider something very serious.

In our justice system, our Supreme Court justices are supposed to be fair and unbiased. However, if this were really the case, then why do we go through such pain-staking efforts to ensure that a particular justice who is appointed to the Supreme Court is a "conservative" or a "liberal?" Who are we fooling?

This transcends into the fact that any legislation that comes out of the Supreme Court, likely will be decided before a case is even heard. If you've got five "conservative" justices and four "liberal" justices, or the reverse, then in advance, can't you guess what the decision will likely be on a particular issue? And why do we know what the outcome will be before the opinion is even read? Simple. Because the Supreme Court is comprised of bias. If an issue went to court today or tomorrow, most would already know the outcome of the case before a decision is even given.

Therefore, are the decisions we receive from this body really justice, or are they just politics as usual, conservative vs. liberal, as they have come to be labeled? And so it seems that We the People, are just giving powerful, lifetime/career appointments to persons who in essence, are no more than politicians. This can have a profoundly negative effect not only on Black America, but America as a whole.

So my point is that in our Constitution, it states that anything the people do not like, or which has become antiquated, the people have the power to change. Maybe, just maybe, we should consider starting to use our power.

ANALOGIES,

EXPERIENCES

& EXAMPLES

What's Important

Can people keep an animal from attacking them if it is hungry? It will be very difficult, and human beings, simply being a higher form of animal, are just like everything else. If primary needs are not cared for, study after study shows very difficult times in getting people to pay attention to morals and family values if their basic needs are not met. This is not to say that these people's morals or values are any less, but who wishes to focus on these things when they are literally at risk of starving?

My point is that we have millions of Americans who believe in working very hard for themselves.

In fact, worker's productivity has increased significantly in the U.S. in the last few years. The problem, however, occurs when these workers are severely exploited, and virtually left to starve. Again and again, many people have come to America with expectations of fair wages for a hard days work. America prided itself on this. But today, Americans are finding it increasingly difficult to provide decent lives for themselves and their families. So not only is this bad, but such a situation will drive individuals to all sorts of atrocities in the U.S., even when this shouldn't be the case.

You see, dozens of economists, lawyers, and businessmen, from a variety of learning institutions all over the world, have repeatedly tried to find a solution. But the truth is that society's problems today, are not necessarily those of academic pursuits. They likely have more to do with humanitarian and religious/God-fearing issues.

Though there are few quick fixes, some serious thinking prompted me to at least one possible small solution. Aside from organizations not developing "treaties" to keep from firing thousands of more workers, which will ultimately lead to the virtual decline of America as we know it, with regard to low-end workers, again, we should increase the current minimum wage to a low *liveable* wage, but nonetheless, a liveable wage. Offset these increases with a reduction in quarterly cash income tax payments for businesses, with perhaps a 1-2% tax incentive thrown in, or again, subsidize the difference. This should offset inflation by holding down higher prices for goods, because of the reduction in cash outlays, thereby leaving net income profit margins in tact. So at the same time, this would thereby increase living standards for present underprivileged individuals, and increase the work force, as many unemployed people today do not even seek work because they have little chance of making a livable wage.

If this initiative were to be successful, this would save us billions of dollars in federal aid (i.e. welfare monies, reduction in welfare personnel, paperwork, printing of food stamps, etc.), creating a situation where we would all win. And besides, when corporations earn hundreds of millions, and even billions of dollars per year in profits, but pay their employees low, minimum wages, this indicates that something is wrong.

Disadvantaged individuals are often characterized as being lazy, and some are. However, the vast number of disadvantaged people are not, and many of these people happen to be very hard working individuals.

I recently encountered individuals who overlooked a sick baby, because it was of the wrong race, and from the wrong neighborhood. However, these same people fought hard against a decent minimum wage not too long ago, and even had the audacity to show up later at a rally dressed as pro-life advocates, attempting eradicate the "sins" of poor, unemployed mothers. Does this make sense to you?

This hints to the fact that we live in a mean, twisted society. And you probably are saying right now, "Tell me something that I don't already know," too. But unfortunately, unless some changes are made, and people such as Newt Gingrich and his gang are held in check, things won't get any better before they get worse--a lot worse. In fact, whether we realize it or not, on the present course we are on, I predict that America as we know it, won't make it beyond three more presidential elections.

The Bully Syndrome

In the past, African-Americans appeared to be allowing history to repeat itself. Blacks seemed to let themselves be bullied, yet would come back for more.

Remember in grade school, when there would always seem to be a bully at every school, and this bully would inevitably seem to pick on those who appeared to be weaker and perhaps less strong than him or her?

Well, there is a moral to this story. Remember how the cycle of bullying would continue, constantly picking on the kid who always seemed to be minding his or her own business? Do you remember what inevitably seemed to happen almost every time? Almost always, the bully would push and push until the apparent weaker kid began to fight back, and often times, the apparent weaker kid would win the fight.

Such is the case with American blacks. And the reason that I state only blacks, is because everyone, sometimes, other blacks even, seem to wish to pick on blacks, because they feel that at least for right now, blacks are the "weaker kid." Besides, who in their right minds would want to fight a lion, knowing that he or she would likely be slain? No one. So, human instinct tells us to do the cowardly thing, and attack the less fortunate--this is true in a social sense, political, you name it, just as in the animal kingdom--and as many proud, wealthy people often quickly point-out today, survival of the fittest, at least while they have an advantage.

No Respect

Now, fearing that such information would open a can of worms, many have historically attempted to keep such information from surfacing--publishers wouldn't publish it, movie makers wouldn't produce films about it, etcetera, etcetera--censorship through pocket veto almost sort-of-speak. And many of these same persons literally scream over the thought of censorship being aimed at them, and say shame on places such as Russia, while they quietly do the same thing.

However, one important fact is that in any civilized society, namely ours, no one will ever benefit from ignorance. Getting back to an earlier chapter, we must confront the truth about race and other issues head-on, for the longer we hold out, the more tense things will become. And one thing that angers people more than anything is keeping things away from them, and lying to them. Perhaps such information could eventually make our country a kinder, gentler place to live, if at least, it is perceived that we are finally beginning to become forthcoming with one another.

Although Black America is in the dark, not yet in the light, I am reminded by an old saying which goes, "It is always darkest before dawn."

The new generation of African-Americans is beginning to see the need to stimulate their own economy--and to some extremes, if not buy black, go without. This mind-set is appearing to be slowly sweeping the nation, as a group with this much economic clout, still gets no respect.

The 90's Women

What is being demonstrated by women in the 1990's should not be a surprise to us. Women, like other minority groups in America, especially African-Americans, have to a large degree, been systematically discriminated against. Lower pay in the labor force, limited to excel in narrow occupations such as human resources... For the most part, women have just been expected to "remain in their places" with regard to important decision making.

The fact is that women, like many minority groups in America, have been oppressed or stifled from excelling in many areas.

Recently, I have heard many men complain about the atrocious behavior of women today, and comment that a revolution is taking place before our very eyes. My response is really? Are we surprised?

We all must understand that in most societies, revolution is good. But on the other hand, rebellion can be very destructive, and subsequently lethal to any society. This may presently be the case in America. But with my saying that, also understand that women cannot bare the brunt or be blamed for their outrage, and aggressive behavior. Many women are simply acting as most human beings in their situations would--rebelling against the oppressors who have kept them from maximizing their potential for many years. Women are saying no more, and I applaud them.

I have great respect and admiration for many of today's women. I myself was virtually raised by a single-parent mother for much of my adolescent and young-adult life. This situation undoubtedly sensitized me to many of women's struggles. I am certainly not saying that I don't disagree with some of what goes on by women in our society, but then again, show me one group that can be considered model perfect.

WHAT BUSINESS CAN LEARN FROM SHAMEFUL HISTORY

Thomas Jefferson summed up America perfectly when he once stated, "We have the wolf by the ear with the issue of slavery. We can neither hold him, nor safely let him go." This is how many white males today feel about blacks in America.

Businesses must be very careful not to be overly consumed with making profits at all costs, as is currently the case, for the outcome is too detrimental--Workers working without health insurance, working for meager wages, etc. Society mustn't be sacrificed just for the sake of retaining more profits, because when society is sacrificed, this also means that America is on the verge of losing too.

Today, all across the nation, you can find middle-class Americans being booted out of the middle-class because of essential corporate greed. And those who have not been booted out, should only give themselves a few more years, when college graduates could even be competing for low-wage jobs at fast-food restaurants, at competitive prices too--$5.00 an hour compared to another's bid at $4.75. But nonetheless, companies and politicians often justify actions with "We must keep pace with the competition..." or "The government shouldn't make laws regulating my business, give that power to the states," or "Let us regulate ourselves."

As these types of arguments permeate our society today, they also once permeated our society more than 130 years ago, almost in duplicate fashion. In fact, virtually these same arguments took us into what is now referred to as the Civil War. People wanted *states* to have the right to govern various activities, so wealthy Southerners could be free to do what they pleased with their negro slaves.

We have so-called responsive politicians today arguing those same views, and one of them of all things even holds a Ph.D in history. So it appears that after all of this time, many persons dressed in cloaks as "Republicans" are seeking to engage into the very debate which once divided a nation. This is very dangerous politics, and should not be taken lightly.

But still not expecting you to form an opinion just yet, let me paint an even more vivid, clearer picture, further enabling you to decide. You see, during the 350 years of the infamous Atlantic Slave Trade, approximately 15 million Africans were transported to the Americas.

However, many back then, as many in business would do today, argued that sea captains did not capture slaves, they simply transported a commodity, and bartered guns, knives, horses, and iron works with native Africans, who actually were the ones who did much of the capturing. "We only supplied people with merchandise," many of these alleged capitalists would argue. But even though these men often sailed from England, which as a nation, eventually transported at least half of all African slaves, the Dutch, Danish, Portuguese, French and Spanish, all profited remarkably from such a despicable industry as well. But as many business person's actions of today would suggest, though a despicable industry, slavery was a business, justifying such actions as okay.

Monsters who would justify an institution such as slavery as a legitimate business should be bound to such an institution for a period of years themselves.

Hearkening unto the understanding and regulations of men, rather than to that of God, as the Bible cautions us, coupled with such above attitudes, perhaps may have something to do with the multiplying and increasing natural disasters our country has witnessed in the past decade.

But anyway, though the Danish and Dutch were of the first to give up the amoral institution/business of slave trading, they later were followed by other major European nations, including England, which came to despise this once profitable industry. America, on the other hand, because of the explosion of the rich cash crop of cotton, proved to be one of the last of the western nations to give up slavery.

Though not widely enforced, the U.S. Congress forbade the importation of slaves after 1808, under the watchful eye of Great Britain, who had ended the practice in 1807, and sought to prevent its continuance in other nations. But nonetheless, until the American Civil War, a thriving illegal slave trade developed in America, because of cotton's great presence in the South.

Nonetheless, however, since slavery had ended in the European nations, after loosing much of its value, by the early 1900's, Great Britain, France, Italy, Belgium, Germany, Portugal and Spain, all had carved up the entire continent of Africa into little pieces for themselves. This was done under what is today referred to as colonialism. These countries used Africa as a natural resources "play ground" for their countries, while offering little but relegating subservient status to blacks. Even after declaring African nations independent, through the unnatural boundaries which were set by the Europeans and colonialism, the many African tribes, with their different languages, different cultures, and sometimes dislikes for other tribes, were forced to live together, and somehow manage to rule themselves, which has resulted in virtual anarchy for many years.

And this so-called "business," despite being despicable, and banned by virtually all nations, as late as the 1950's, still caused the United Nations to receive complaints that a thriving trade in African slaves on the Arabian peninsula was still a regular occurrence.

But besides these facts being informational, the point is that what essentially set-out to be for reasons of "business," gravely amoral practices have often taken place for the mere sake of profits--leaving behind destruction and mayhem. Today, this is seemingly once again the case, with the erosion of the American middle-class, during companies' quest to make more profits.

This is a warning to individual private citizens, and leaders of both business and political institutions, that the continued arguments of states deciding much of what goes on in America, will ultimately fractionalize and divide our country. Though my warnings may be imprudently ignored, such a continued political push will undoubtedly lead to a sad, sad state in American history.

Though it may even take a decade to realize the effects, history has already indicated to us the outcome. Hence, if states do not engage in one individual, unstabalizing practice, sending America into ten different, conflicting directions, states will ultimately engage in another unsavory practice, ultimately making America weaker and weaker as we go along.

But my last point, however, is this. Though we no longer see the Ku Klux Klan running around in sheets, we know that many of these people have traded in their sheets for suits, and now call themselves non-racist, Republicans, such as David Duke. In fact, many of these people help to comprise what is called the "Christian Right."

But anyway, if one of our most influential leaders has a Ph.D in history, and knows of the horrible fates associated with what he of all people is proposing, then what could possibly be his ulterior motives for what he is proposing?

The Bible tells us that one day, a charismatic leader will come along, preaching peace, but will deliver nothing but despair and destruction. This is not to label anyone as an Anti-Christ, however, it is to state that Americans must thoroughly question the motives of our political leaders, rather than being gullible, or simply taking these leader's words at face value. Our country could slip into a living Hell if we do that, making us a docile people, and as history teaches us, a docile people usually becomes an enslaved people.

Summary

Business leaders must not be so shallow that profits are one of the only things that are considered. The big picture must be weighed at all times, meaning that if the big picture will be unfavorable, then proposed actions should not be undertaken. Some would call this being visionary, asking oneself what effects will these actions have on the future, as opposed to concentrating on the here and now, like many organizations today in America. Minor day-to-day initiatives ultimately, often proves inconsequential once the big picture day arrives. Or summing it up another way, though the battle may be important, it should not be sacrificed at the cost of losing the war.

The layoffs of millions of Americans, which in one report was more than 4,000 layoffs daily, has people scared of not being able to work and feed their families. This is so as many companies bear little responsibility in being concerned with what these once faithful employees will do once let go, and their severance pay runs out. This simply is not right.

So, as mass corporate layoffs are of a major detrimental consequence to the favorable, long-term, big picture for America, they must be halted one way or another, for they are drastically contributing to America's present crash course with decline.

Whⱥt The Future Holds

Before the arrival of the English, Native Americans lived in peace and harmony for more than 400 years. There were more than 17 million Native Americans, comprising different tribes while living in today's United States. However, today, that number is barely 2 million, including Eskimos in Alaska.

But anyway, The Haudenoshonee Indian Nation, which resided in upper-state New York when English colonists first arrived, had devised a government which was deemed brilliant. In fact, this government was so brilliant, that Benjamin Franklin, while visiting this tribe, returned to Philadelphia to help form the present U.S. government, modeled after the Haudenoshonee form of government.

However, after the newly arrived English set its sights on capitalism, in a very short period of time, more than 400 years of peace among the Haudenoshonee Nation was ruined, forever.

Animals which were once shared and hunted only to provide food and clothing, upon a few years after English fur traders arrived in the Ohio River Valley, were extinct, and also, during and around that time, tribes which had been peaceful for centuries, started warring against one another.

This is stated because, while capitalism has its benefits, the above example is to illustrate the havoc in which capitalism can bring if not performed in moderation. So as such, I believe that America potentially can have a bright future, however, this depends almost entirely upon its people. For as things stand presently, on automatic pilot, it is doubtful that our country will withstand three more presidential elections.

So nonetheless, obviously, some changes will have to be made to brighten our future. I predicted that President Clinton would be elected in 1992, and I also predict that he will be re-elected in 1996. And after analyzing the situation, I think this will be good for the country as a whole. But on the other hand, I am not sure how much longer Republicans will continue to dominate. One thing I do know, however, is that their current methods will not keep them in office for very long.

Basically, people do not trust politicians right now, period, Democrats or Republicans. But whether or not a third party is the cure for us, I am still not yet quite convinced. The reasons are largely due to campaign financing, as things are currently.

Blacks and whites will likely finally begin to share some common ground, as many whites, due to new-found experiences, will likely be humbled, and will answer the call-to-action for better race relations.

In a nutshell, the author believes that blacks and whites can and will get along, but the author is not confident that 100% absolute integration will ever be the case, either. However, the author is becoming more and more convinced that a "fair" or moderate amount of integration and "segregation" will ultimately be more acceptable, as people with few insignificant differences, ultimately will still need their space, sort of like a husband or wife needing his or her space, sort-of-speak. These two can love one another, and live in perfect harmony, but they shouldn't smother one another either. Now, I am not even remotely suggesting that separate but equal is or should be our future, but, I do suggest that moderate integration will be the best hope that we've got. And this will likely work beautifully, as long as one group doesn't try to stifle or oppress the other.

Summary

There is a moral to this story. For all Bible believing, God fearing people, we should note that when one compares the hostility and treatment of blacks in American society, to the Israelites in Ancient Egypt, there appears to be but few if any differences.

And also, if one remembers the great Empire of Egypt, then one would also remember that shortly after the liberation of the Israelites from Egypt, Egypt fell. My statements are not to suggest anything, however, these are intriguing facts.

No one really knows if America is on its last leg, but history does repeat itself, again and again. And internal conflict has ultimately led to the demise of virtually each great civilization. One can look no further than to the school age story of Julius Caesar, the man betrayed by his own for the reasons of greed and jealousy. Sound familiar?

Responsible businesses will undoubtedly be needed to help bridge crossroads in America, as businesses have the resources, and quick responsive capabilities to help get us back on track. But if we allow companies to carry too much greed, and too much power over citizens, then we can certainly end up "cutting-off our noses, to spite our own faces," hint, hint.

LETTERS TO THE AUTHOR

If you have questions or comments, you can write to the author at

P.O. Box 3075, Little Rock, Arkansas 72203.

INDEX